W9-BIA-995

VOLUME 2

DIABETIC LIVING® EVERYDAY COOKING IS
PART OF A BOOK SERIES PUBLISHED BY
BETTER HOMES AND GARDENS SPECIAL
INTEREST MEDIA, DES MOINES, IOWA

Soft Chocolate Chip Cookies
recipe, page 147

(letter from the editor)

What can I eat? When you have diabetes, that's a thought that comes up every day—and every meal. To control my weight and balance my medications (I use insulin), I need to know just how many carbohydrates my food choices contain. That's why all of our recipes include a nutrition analysis as well as diabetic exchanges and carb choices.

As a person with type 1 diabetes, I know that nutritious food helps me control my condition and feel good. That's why I appreciate this collection of healthful, lightened recipes that I can count on to fit my meal plan and nourish my family. Because the Better Homes and Gardens Test Kitchen® has perfected every recipe, I know each dish will give me good results and taste delicious. "This doesn't taste like a diabetic recipe. It's yummy!" is what we hear at *Diabetic Living* taste panels.

The registered dietitians in our Test Kitchen design each recipe to deliver healthful amounts of calories, carbs, and sodium. Because they know you and I don't want to deprive ourselves, they make sure the serving sizes are ample and satisfying. They also keep an eye on the ingredients—not too many or too exotic. And they try to use healthful convenience foods, such as reduced-sodium chicken broth and whole grain bread, whenever possible.

This collection will help you spend less time worrying about what to eat and more time savoring easy, at-home cooking with your family. From Family-Pleasing Dinners, *page 6,* to Good-for-You Snacks, *page 116,* there's a recipe for every meal. I hope many recipes from this book will become family favorites all week long.

Kelly Rawlings

Kelly Rawlings, editor
Diabetic Living® magazine

ON THE COVER: Blueberry-Mango Upside-Down Cake (recipe, page 142). Photographer: Pete Krumhardt. Food stylist: Nicole Faber.

Editor in Chief DEBORAH GORE OHRN
Creative Director BRIDGET SANDQUIST

Art Director MICHELLE BILYEU
Editor KELLY RAWLINGS

Contributing Editor SHELLI MCCONNELL
Contributing Designer JILL BUDDEN
Contributing Copy Editor GRETCHEN KAUFFMAN
Contributing Proofreader CARRIE SCHMITZ
Test Kitchen Director LYNN BLANCHARD
Test Kitchen Product Supervisor LAURA MARZEN, R.D.
Editorial Assistants LORI EGGERS, MARLENE TODD
Business Office Assistant SHARON LEIN

EDITORIAL ADMINISTRATION

Managing Editor KATHLEEN ARMENTROUT
Copy Chief DOUG KOUMA
Office Manager CINDY SLOBASZEWSKI
Senior Copy Editors ELIZABETH KEEST SEDREL, JENNIFER SPEER RAMUNDT

EDITORIAL SERVICES

Color/Quality Manager DALE TUNENDER
Photo Studio Manager JEFF ANDERSON
Color/Quality Analyst HEIDI PARCEL
Prepress Desktop Specialist KRISTIN E. REESE

CONSUMER MARKETING

Vice President, Consumer Marketing DAVE BALL
Consumer Products Marketing Director STEVE SWANSON
Consumer Products Marketing Manager WENDY MERICAL
Senior Business Manager TODD VOSS
Production Director DOUGLAS M. JOHNSTON

MEREDITH PUBLISHING GROUP

President JACK GRIFFIN
President, Better Homes and Gardens ANDY SAREYAN
Editorial Director MIKE LAFAVORE **Finance and Administration** MIKE RIGG
Manufacturing BRUCE HESTON **Corporate Sales** JACK BAMBERGER
Interactive Media LAUREN WIENER **Corporate Marketing** NANCY WEBER
Research BRITTA WARE **Chief Technology Officer** TINA STEIL
New Media Marketing Services ANDY WILSON

President and Chief Executive Officer STEPHEN M. LACY

Chairman of the Board WILLIAM T. KERR

In Memoriam — E.T. MEREDITH III (1933-2003)

Diabetic Living Everyday Cooking is part of a series published by Meredith Corp., 1716 Locust St., Des Moines, IA 50309-3023.

If you have comments or questions about the editorial material in *Diabetic Living Everyday Cooking*, write to the editor of *Diabetic Living* magazine, Meredith Corp., 1716 Locust St., Des Moines, IA 50309-3023. Send an e-mail to diabeticliving@meredith.com or call 800/678-2651. *Diabetic Living* magazine is available by subscription or on the newsstand. To order a subscription to *Diabetic Living* magazine, go to *DiabeticLivingOnline.com*.

First edition. Printed in U.S.A.

ISSN 1943-2615 ISBN 978-0-696-24255-7

contents

Sweet 'n' Salty Snack Mix,
recipe, page 124

family-pleasing dinners

Margarita-Glazed Pork Chops

If you're looking for some new fresh and flavorful entrées to add to your weekly mix, turn to these soon-to-be family favorites. You'll find an assortment of grilled, slow-cooked, baked, steamed, and stir-fried specialities, all bursting with great taste and packed with good nutrition.

Margarita-Glazed Pork Chops

When the chops are grilled to perfection, succulent juices lock in, creating a burst of flavor with each bite.

PER SERVING: 184 cal., 3 g total fat (1 g sat. fat), 62 mg chol., 211 mg sodium, 8 g carb., 0 g fiber, 26 g pro. Exchanges: 0.5 carb., 3.5 very lean meat. Carb choices: 0.5.

- **4 boneless pork top loin chops, cut ¾ inch thick (1 to 1½ pounds total)**
- **⅓ cup low-sugar orange marmalade**
- **1 fresh jalapeño chile pepper, seeded and finely chopped***
- **2 tablespoons tequila or lime juice**
- **½ teaspoon grated fresh ginger or ¼ teaspoon ground ginger**
- **¼ cup snipped fresh cilantro**

1. Trim fat from pork. For glaze, in a small bowl, stir together orange marmalade, chile pepper, tequila, and ginger.

2. For a charcoal grill, place chops on the grill rack directly over medium coals. Grill, uncovered, for 7 to 9 minutes or until no pink remains (160°F) and juices run clear, turning once halfway through grilling and spooning glaze over chops frequently during the last 2 minutes of grilling. (For a gas grill, preheat grill. Reduce heat to medium. Place chops on grill rack over heat. Cover and grill as above.)

3. To serve, sprinkle pork chops with cilantro. **Makes 4 servings.**

***Test Kitchen Tip:** Because chile peppers contain volatile oils that can burn your skin and eyes, avoid direct contact with them as much as possible. When working with chile peppers, wear plastic or rubber gloves. If your bare hands do touch the peppers, wash your hands and nails well with soap and warm water.

Pork with Mushrooms

Use an assortment of fresh mushrooms in this quick-to-fix pan sauce.

PER SERVING: 319 cal., 12 g total fat (3 g sat. fat), 95 mg chol., 386 mg sodium, 9 g carb., 1 g fiber, 36 g pro. Exchanges: 1 vegetable, 4.5 lean meat. Carb choices: 0.5.

- **2 tablespoons olive oil**
- **1 pound fresh mushrooms (such as stemmed shiitake, cremini, and/or button), sliced**
- **½ cup finely chopped onion**
- **6 cloves garlic, minced**
- **1 tablespoon snipped fresh thyme or ½ teaspoon dried thyme, crushed**
- **½ cup dry white wine or reduced-sodium chicken broth**
- **1 tablespoon grated Parmesan cheese**
- **¼ teaspoon salt**
- **¼ teaspoon ground black pepper**
- **4 boneless pork loin chops, cut ¾ inch thick (about 1¼ pounds total)**
- **1 cup reduced-sodium chicken broth**

1. In a large skillet, heat 1 tablespoon of the oil over medium-high heat. Add mushrooms; cook about 5 minutes or until tender and starting to brown, stirring occasionally. Add onion; cook and stir about 4 minutes or until onion is tender. Add the garlic and thyme; cook and stir for 1 minute more. Carefully add wine to skillet. Bring to boiling; reduce heat. Boil gently, uncovered, for 2 to 3 minutes or until most of the liquid has evaporated. Remove from heat; transfer to a medium bowl. Stir in Parmesan cheese, ⅛ teaspoon of the salt, and ⅛ teaspoon of the pepper.

2. Season chops with the remaining ⅛ teaspoon salt and the remaining ⅛ teaspoon pepper. In the same skillet, heat the remaining 1 tablespoon oil over medium-high heat. Add chops; cook for 6 minutes, turning once to brown evenly. Add mushroom mixture and broth to skillet around the chops. Bring to boiling; reduce heat. Cover and simmer for 7 to 10 minutes or until no pink remains (160°F) and juices run clear. Transfer chops to a serving platter; cover and keep warm.

3. Bring mushroom mixture in skillet to boiling; reduce heat. Boil gently, uncovered, for 5 minutes. Spoon some of the mushroom mixture over chops; pass remaining mushroom mixture. **Makes 4 servings (1 chop with ½ cup mushroom sauce per serving).**

Pork with Mushrooms

Mediterranean Pork Chops

These herb-rubbed roasted chops pair well with a green salad and an array of roasted veggies.

PER SERVING: 161 cal., 5 g total fat (2 g sat. fat), 62 mg chol., 192 mg sodium, 1 g carb., 0 g fiber, 25 g pro. Exchanges: 3.5 very lean meat, 1 fat. Carb choices: 0.

- **4 boneless or bone-in pork loin chops, cut ½ inch thick (1 to 1½ pounds total)**
- **¼ teaspoon salt**
- **¼ teaspoon freshly ground black pepper**
- **1 tablespoon finely snipped fresh rosemary or 1 teaspoon dried rosemary, crushed**
- **3 cloves garlic, minced**

1. Preheat oven to 425°F. Sprinkle all sides of chops with salt and pepper; set aside. In a small bowl, combine rosemary and garlic. Sprinkle rosemary mixture evenly over all sides of the chops; rub in with your fingers.

2. Place chops on a rack in a shallow roasting pan. Roast chops for 10 minutes. Reduce oven temperature to 350°F and continue roasting about 25 minutes or until no pink remains (160°F) and juices run clear. **Makes 4 servings.**

(naturally healthful)

Many fresh pork products are enhanced with a water-salt solution to tenderize the meat. While enhanced pork products have similar levels of calories to natural pork products, they can contribute unnecessary and unhealthful levels of sodium to your diet.

It can be tricky to find pork that hasn't been treated, but with a little label-reading savvy, you can zero in on the fresh cuts. Look for terms such as "natural," "all natural," or "simply natural" to avoid added sodium. And stay clear of products with terms such as "extra-tender," "deep-basted," or "self-basting."

Mediterranean Pork Chops

Latin-Spiced
Pork Tenderloins

Quick Tip:

Tender cuts of pork such as boneless top loin chops, bone-in loin chops, loin roasts, and tenderloins cook best when using dry heat. These methods include broiling, grilling, pan-broiling, pan-frying, stir-frying, and roasting.

Latin-Spiced Pork Tenderloins

If you have leftovers, roll slices of this spice-covered meat in a whole wheat tortilla along with shredded carrots, sliced jalapeño chile peppers, and snipped fresh cilantro.

PER SERVING: 138 cal., 3 g total fat (1 g sat. fat), 73 mg chol., 198 mg sodium, 1 g carb., 0 g fiber, 24 g pro. Exchanges: 3.5 very lean meat, 0.5 fat. Carb choices: 0.

2 teaspoons chili powder
1 teaspoon garlic powder
1 teaspoon dried oregano, crushed
½ teaspoon salt
½ teaspoon ground black pepper
½ teaspoon ground cumin
¼ teaspoon cayenne pepper
2 1-pound pork tenderloins

1. Preheat oven to 425°F. For rub, in a small bowl, combine chili powder, garlic powder, oregano, salt, black pepper, cumin, and cayenne pepper. Sprinkle rub evenly over all sides of tenderloins; rub in with your fingers.

2. Place tenderloins on a rack in a shallow roasting pan. Roast for 25 to 35 minutes or until an instant-read thermometer inserted into thickest part of the tenderloins registers 155°F.

3. Remove tenderloins from oven. Cover tightly with foil; let stand for 15 minutes before slicing. The temperature of the meat after standing should be 160°F. **Makes 8 servings.**

Asian-Style Pork Steaks

Round out the meal with carrots, snow peas, and radishes.

PER SERVING: 173 cal., 6 g total fat (2 g sat. fat), 73 mg chol., 349 mg sodium, 3 g carb., 0 g fiber, 23 g pro. Exchanges: 3.5 lean meat. Carb choices: 0.

2 pork shoulder steaks, cut ¾ inch thick (1 to 1¼ pounds total)
¼ cup reduced-sodium soy sauce
¼ cup dry red wine
¼ cup lemon juice
2 tablespoons chopped onion
1½ teaspoons grated fresh ginger or ½ teaspoon ground ginger
2 cloves garlic, minced
¼ teaspoon ground black pepper

1. Place pork in a resealable plastic bag set in a shallow dish. For the marinade, in a small bowl, stir together soy sauce, wine, lemon juice, onion, ginger, garlic, and pepper. Pour marinade over pork in bag. Seal bag; turn to coat pork. Marinate in the refrigerator for 4 to 24 hours, turning bag occasionally.

2. Drain pork, discarding marinade. For a charcoal grill, place pork on the grill rack directly over medium coals. Grill, uncovered, for 12 to 15 minutes or until no pink remains (160°F) and juices run clear, turning once halfway through grilling. (For a gas grill, preheat grill. Reduce heat to medium. Place pork on grill rack over heat. Cover and grill as above.)

3. To serve, cut pork steaks in half. **Makes 4 servings.**

Asian-Style Pork Steaks

Cilantro-Lime Flank Steak

Make sure you use a sharp knife for scoring the steak.

PER SERVING: 203 cal., 9 g total fat (3 g sat. fat), 47 mg chol., 250 mg sodium, 5 g carb., 1 g fiber, 26 g pro. Exchanges: 4 lean meat. Carb choices: 0.

- **1 pound beef flank steak**
- **¼ cup water**
- **¼ cup lime juice**
- **6 cloves garlic, minced**
- **2 tablespoons snipped fresh cilantro**
- **2 teaspoons snipped fresh oregano or ½ teaspoon dried oregano, crushed**
- **¼ teaspoon ground chipotle chile powder or regular chili powder**
- **¼ teaspoon salt**
- **⅛ teaspoon ground black pepper**
- **1 cup Avocado-Poblano Pico de Gallo (see recipe, below)**

1. Trim fat from steak. Score both sides of steak in a diamond pattern by making shallow diagonal cuts at 1-inch intervals. Place steak in a resealable plastic bag set in a shallow dish. For marinade, in a small bowl, combine the water, lime juice, garlic, cilantro, oregano, and chipotle chile powder. Pour over steak in bag. Seal bag; turn to coat steak. Marinate in the refrigerator for 1 to 2 hours, turning bag occasionally.

2. Drain steak, reserving marinade. Sprinkle steak with salt and black pepper. For a charcoal grill, place steak on the grill rack directly over medium coals. Grill, uncovered, for 17 to 21 minutes or until medium doneness (160°F), turning once and brushing with the reserved marinade halfway through grilling. Discard any remaining marinade. (For a gas grill, preheat grill. Reduce heat to medium. Place steak on grill rack over heat. Cover and grill as above.)

3. To serve, thinly slice steak across the grain; divide among four serving plates. Top with Avocado-Poblano Pico de Gallo. If desired, garnish with *lime wedges* and *cilantro*. **Makes 4 servings.**

Avocado-Poblano Pico de Gallo: Preheat broiler. Place 1 fresh poblano chile pepper or green sweet pepper and 1 yellow or red sweet pepper on a baking sheet lined with foil. Broil 4 inches from the heat for 7 to 10 minutes or until skins are bubbly and blackened, turning occasionally. Carefully bring the foil up and around the peppers to enclose. Let stand 15 minutes or until cool enough to handle. Pull skins off gently and slowly using a paring knife;* discard. Remove pepper stems, seeds, and membranes; chop the peppers. In a bowl, combine chopped peppers; 1 medium tomato, chopped; ⅓ cup chopped red onion; 2 tablespoons snipped fresh cilantro; ½ teaspoon finely shredded lime peel; 1 tablespoon lime juice; and ¼ teaspoon salt. Gently toss to combine. Stir in 1 small avocado, halved, pitted, peeled, and chopped.

***Test Kitchen Tip:** Because chile peppers contain volatile oils that can burn your skin and eyes, avoid direct contact with them as much as possible. When working with chile peppers, wear plastic or rubber gloves. If your bare hands do touch the peppers, wash your hands and nails well with soap and warm water.

Asian Flank Steak

Dinner will be minutes away if you assemble the sauce mixture and start the steak marinating the night before.

PER SERVING: 205 cal., 9 g total fat (4 g sat. fat), 46 mg chol., 419 mg sodium, 5 g carb., 0 g fiber, 26 g pro. Exchanges: 3.5 lean meat. Carb choices: 0.

- **1 1½-pound beef flank steak**
- **¼ cup lower-sodium beef broth**
- **3 tablespoons bottled hoisin sauce**
- **2 tablespoons reduced-sodium soy sauce**
- **1 green onion, thinly sliced**
- **1 tablespoon dry sherry (optional)**
- **½ teaspoon grated fresh ginger**
- **2 cloves garlic, minced**

1. Trim fat from steak. Score both sides of steak in a diamond pattern by making diagonal cuts at 1-inch intervals. Place steak in a resealable plastic bag set in a shallow dish. For marinade, in a small bowl, combine broth, hoisin sauce, soy sauce, green onion, sherry (if desired), ginger, and garlic. Pour over steak in bag. Seal bag; turn to coat steak. Marinate in refrigerator for 2 to 24 hours, turning bag occasionally.

2. Drain steak, discarding marinade. For a charcoal grill, place steak on the grill rack directly over medium coals. Grill, uncovered, for 17 to 21 minutes or until medium doneness (160°F), turning once halfway through grilling. (For a gas grill, preheat grill. Reduce heat to medium. Place steak on grill rack over heat. Cover and grill as above.) To serve, thinly slice steak across the grain. **Makes 6 servings.**

Cilantro-Lime Flank Steak

(10 quick fillings)

When you have leftover tortillas, choose one of these tasty fillings for a fast wrap.

1. **Spread** on a little fat-free cream cheese and top with sweet pepper strips, red onion slices, and crisp cucumber slices.
2. **Layer** with slices of Muenster cheese, spring greens, thinly sliced roasted turkey, and dried cranberries.
3. **Stir** a little prepared horseradish into some light mayonnaise. Then drizzle it over layers of thinly sliced roasted beef and fresh arugula.
4. **Top** with some shredded deli-roasted chicken, a spoonful of bottled salsa, and a few avocado slices.
5. **Try** some leaf lettuce topped with tuna salad and halved grape tomatoes.
6. **Slice** some leftover grilled steak and add roasted red sweet peppers and fresh baby spinach.
7. **Scramble** a couple of eggs or egg whites and top with a spoonful of fresh salsa and light dairy sour cream.
8. **Roast** a few of your favorite vegetables and wrap up with a slice of your favorite reduced-fat cheese.
9. **Spoon** on some purchased chicken salad and top with fresh peach slices and toasted almonds.
10. **Slather** on almond butter and add sliced bananas or apples.

Beef and Chipotle Burritos

Beef and Chipotle Burritos

Chances are you'll have leftover chipotle peppers. Freeze the smoky peppers and sauce for another use.

PER SERVING: 308 cal., 9 g total fat (3 g sat. fat), 62 mg chol., 482 mg sodium, 24 g carb., 12 g fiber, 30 g pro. Exchanges: 1 vegetable, 1 starch, 3.5 lean meat. Carb choices: 1.5.

- **1 recipe Pico de Gallo Salsa (see recipe, below)**
- **1½ pounds boneless beef round steak, cut ¾ inch thick**
- **2 14.5-ounce cans no-salt-added diced tomatoes, undrained**
- **1 small onion, chopped**
- **2 canned chipotle chile peppers in adobo sauce, finely chopped***
- **3 cloves garlic, minced**
- **1 teaspoon dried oregano, crushed**
- **¼ teaspoon ground cumin**
- **8 7- to 8-inch whole wheat flour tortillas, warmed**
- **½ cup shredded reduced-fat cheddar cheese (2 ounces)**

1. Prepare Pico de Gallo Salsa. Trim fat from steak. Cut steak into six pieces. Place steak in a 3½- or 4-quart slow cooker. Add undrained tomatoes, onion, chile peppers, garlic, oregano, and cumin.

2. Cover and cook on low-heat setting for 8 to 10 hours or on high-heat setting for 4 to 5 hours.

3. Using a slotted spoon, transfer meat and tomatoes to a large bowl; reserve cooking liquid in slow cooker. Using two forks, pull meat apart into shreds. Stir enough of the reserved cooking liquid into meat to moisten.

4. To serve, spoon meat mixture just below centers of tortillas. Top with cheese and Pico de Gallo Salsa. Roll up tortillas. **Makes 8 servings.**

Pico de Gallo Salsa: In a small bowl, combine 1 cup finely chopped tomatoes; 2 tablespoons finely chopped onion; 2 tablespoons snipped fresh cilantro; and 1 fresh serrano chile pepper, seeded and finely chopped.* Stir in ½ cup chopped, peeled jicama and ¼ cup radishes cut into thin bite-size strips. Cover and chill until ready to serve.

***Test Kitchen Tip:** Because chile peppers contain volatile oils that can burn your skin and eyes, avoid direct contact with them as much as possible. When working with chile peppers, wear plastic or rubber gloves. If your bare hands do touch the peppers, wash your hands and nails well with soap and warm water.

Beef with Cucumber Raita

Beef with Cucumber Raita

Raita, a yogurt-and-veggie condiment common in Indian cuisine, has a cooling effect on the sizzling steak.

PER SERVING: 176 cal., 5 g total fat (2 g sat. fat), 48 mg chol., 252 mg sodium, 4 g carb., 0 g fiber, 28 g pro. Exchanges: 4 very lean meat, 1 fat. Carb choices: 0.

- **1 6-ounce carton plain fat-free or low-fat yogurt**
- **¼ cup coarsely shredded cucumber**
- **1 tablespoon finely chopped red onion**
- **1 tablespoon snipped fresh mint**
- **¼ teaspoon sugar**
- **¼ teaspoon salt**
- **⅛ teaspoon ground black pepper**
- **1 pound boneless beef sirloin steak, cut 1 inch thick**
- **½ teaspoon Greek seasoning**

1. For raita, in a small bowl, combine yogurt, cucumber, red onion, mint, sugar, salt, and pepper; set aside.

2. Trim fat from steak. Sprinkle steak with Greek seasoning. For a charcoal grill, place steak on the grill rack directly over medium coals. Grill, uncovered, until desired doneness, turning once halfway through grilling. Allow 15 to 17 minutes for medium-rare doneness (145°F) or 20 to 22 minutes for medium doneness (160°F). (For a gas grill, preheat grill. Reduce heat to medium. Place steak on grill rack over heat. Cover; grill as above.)

3. To serve, thinly slice steak across the grain. Serve sliced steak with raita. **Makes 4 servings.**

Tropical Fiesta Steak

Pickapeppa Sauce is a tart-sweet, slightly hot seasoning mixture from Jamaica. Look for it in the condiment aisle at the supermarket.

PER SERVING: 211 cal., 7 g total fat (2 g sat. fat), 48 mg chol., 166 mg sodium, 10 g carb., 1 g fiber, 26 g pro. Exchanges: 0.5 fruit, 3.5 lean meat. Carb choices: 0.5.

- **⅓ cup mango, pear, or apricot nectar**
- **¼ cup snipped fresh mint or basil or 1 tablespoon dried mint, crushed**
- **¼ cup sliced green onions**
- **3 tablespoons Pickapeppa Sauce or spicy brown mustard**
- **1 tablespoon cooking oil**
- **1 tablespoon lemon juice**
- **⅛ teaspoon salt**
- **Several dashes bottled hot pepper sauce**
- **1 1-pound boneless beef top sirloin steak, cut 1 inch thick**
- **½ cup chopped red sweet pepper**
- **½ cup chopped red apple or pear**
- **½ cup chopped peeled mango, unpeeled peach, or unpeeled nectarine**
- **¼ cup sliced celery**

1. For marinade, in a small bowl, stir together nectar, mint, 2 tablespoons of the green onions, the Pickapeppa Sauce, oil, lemon juice, salt, and hot pepper sauce. Remove ¼ cup of the marinade; cover and chill until serving time.

2. Trim fat from steak. Place steak in a resealable plastic bag set in a shallow dish. Pour remaining marinade over steak in bag. Seal bag; turn to coat steak. Marinate in the refrigerator for 12 to 24 hours, turning bag occasionally.

3. For fruit relish, in a small bowl, combine sweet pepper, apple, mango, celery, and the remaining 2 tablespoons green onions. Cover and chill for up to 24 hours.

4. Drain steak, discarding marinade. For a charcoal grill, place steak on the grill rack directly over medium coals. Grill, uncovered, until desired doneness, turning once halfway through grilling. Allow 14 to 18 minutes for medium-rare doneness (145°F) or 18 to 22 minutes for medium doneness (160°F). (For a gas grill, preheat grill. Reduce heat to medium. Place steak on grill rack over heat. Cover and grill as above.)

5. To serve, thinly slice steak across the grain. Serve with fruit relish and drizzle with the reserved ¼ cup marinade. **Makes 4 servings.**

Tropical Fiesta Steak

(gingerly speaking)

Ginger is a semitropical plant that adds a spicy-sweet flavor to recipes. The two most common forms of ginger are fresh as a root and dried and ground as a powder. Look for fresh ginger (also known as gingerroot) in the produce section of your supermarket. Choose a piece that is almost hard with an unwrinkled skin. Use a vegetable peeler to remove the skin before shredding with a fine-grate Microplane. To store, place fresh ginger in a resealable plastic bag and chill for up to 2 months or freeze for longer storage. Purchase ground ginger as you do other spices.

Beef-Broccoli Stir-Fry

Brown rice is a good alternative to the noodles.

PER SERVING: 260 cal., 6 g total fat (1 g sat. fat), 36 mg chol., 539 mg sodium, 31 g carb., 4 g fiber, 24 g pro. Exchanges: 1 vegetable, 1.5 starch, 2.5 very lean meat, 0.5 fat. Carb choices: 2.

¾ cup lower-sodium beef broth
2 tablespoons reduced-sodium soy sauce
1 tablespoon rice vinegar or white vinegar
2 teaspoons cornstarch
2 teaspoons grated fresh ginger or ½ teaspoon ground ginger
2 cloves garlic, minced
¼ teaspoon crushed red pepper
1 pound broccoli
1 pound boneless beef top sirloin steak
2 teaspoons canola oil
2 medium carrots, sliced
4 green onions, sliced
6 ounces dried soba (buckwheat noodles) or multigrain spaghetti, cooked according to package directions

1. For sauce, in a small bowl, combine broth, soy sauce, vinegar, cornstarch, ginger, garlic, and crushed red pepper; set aside. Cut broccoli florets from stems. If desired, peel stems. Cut stems into ¼-inch-thick slices. Set aside. Trim fat from steak. Cut steak across the grain into thin slices; set aside.

2. In a wok or large skillet, heat 1 teaspoon of the oil over medium-high heat. Add broccoli and carrots. Stir-fry 5 to 6 minutes or until crisp-tender; remove from wok.

3. Add the remaining 1 teaspoon oil to hot wok or skillet. Add beef. Stir-fry for 2 to 3 minutes or until desired doneness. Push beef from center of wok or skillet. Stir sauce; add to wok or skillet. Cook and stir until thickened and bubbly. Return vegetables to wok or skillet; add green onions. Stir to coat all ingredients with sauce. Cook and stir until heated through.

4. Serve beef mixture over hot cooked soba or spaghetti. **Makes 6 servings (about 1½ cups per serving).**

Beef-Broccoli Stir-Fry

Saucy Meatballs

You can give this hearty sauce an Italian, Mexican, or Cajun spin by varying the seasoning and type of tomatoes you choose.

PER SERVING: 244 cal., 11 g total fat (3 g sat. fat), 143 mg chol., 604 mg sodium, 14 g carb., 3 g fiber, 24 g pro. Exchanges: 0.5 vegetable, 0.5 starch, 3 lean meat, 0.5 fat. Carb choices: 1.

- **⅓ cup water**
- **¼ cup bulgur**
- **1 egg**
- **1 teaspoon dried Italian seasoning, chili powder, or salt-free Cajun seasoning**
- **¼ teaspoon salt**
- **⅛ teaspoon ground black pepper**
- **1 pound uncooked ground turkey or 90% or higher lean ground beef**
- **1 14.5-ounce can Italian-, Mexican-, or Cajun-style stewed tomatoes, undrained and cut up**
- **2 cups hot cooked spaghetti squash (optional)**
- **2 tablespoons small fresh basil or cilantro leaves or thinly sliced green onion**

1. In a large microwave-safe bowl, combine the water and bulgur. Microwave on 100% power (high) for 1 minute; do not drain. Cool slightly.

2. Stir egg, desired seasoning, salt, and pepper into bulgur mixture. Add ground turkey or beef; mix well. Shape into 24 meatballs. Place in a microwave-safe 2-quart square baking dish. Cover with vented plastic wrap. Microwave on 100% power (high) for 4 minutes, rearranging once; drain off liquid.

Saucy Meatballs over spaghetti squash

3. Pour undrained stewed tomatoes over meatballs. Cover with vented plastic wrap. Microwave on 100% power (high) for 1 to 3 minutes more or until meatballs are no longer pink in centers (165°F).* If desired, serve meatballs over spaghetti squash. Sprinkle with basil, cilantro, or green onion. **Makes 4 servings.**

***Test Kitchen Tip:** Low-wattage microwave ovens may require more time, and high-wattage microwave ovens may require less time.

Greek Pita Pizzas

This trimmed-down beef or lamb pizza features some of the hallmarks of Greek cooking: rosemary, pita bread, feta cheese, and kalamata olives.

PER SERVING: 255 cal., 8 g total fat (4 g sat. fat), 38 mg chol., 432 mg sodium, 28 g carb., 4 g fiber, 16 g pro. Exchanges: 0.5 vegetable, 1.5 starch, 1.5 medium-fat meat. Carb choices: 2.

- **6 ounces lean ground beef or lamb**
- **¼ cup finely chopped onion**
- **2 cloves garlic, minced**
- **1 8-ounce can no-salt-added tomato sauce**
- **1 teaspoon snipped fresh rosemary or ¼ teaspoon dried rosemary, crushed**
- **2 6-inch whole wheat or white pita bread rounds**
- **½ cup shredded part-skim mozzarella cheese (2 ounces)**
- **½ cup shredded fresh spinach**
- **1 small tomato, seeded and chopped**
- **¼ cup crumbled reduced-fat feta cheese (1 ounce)**
- **12 pitted kalamata or ripe olives, quartered (optional)**

1. Preheat oven to 400°F. In a medium nonstick skillet, cook ground beef, onion, and garlic until meat is browned; drain off fat. Stir tomato sauce and rosemary into meat mixture in skillet. Bring to boiling; reduce heat. Simmer, uncovered, for 2 minutes.

2. Carefully split pita bread rounds in half horizontally; place pita halves, rough sides up, on a large baking sheet. Bake for 3 to 4 minutes or until lightly toasted.

3. Top toasted pita bread with meat mixture; sprinkle with mozzarella cheese. Bake for 2 to 3 minutes more or until cheese is melted. Remove from oven. Top with spinach, tomato, feta cheese, and, if desired, olives; serve immediately. **Makes 4 servings.**

Greek Pita Pizzas

(lean labels)

Ground beef can be purchased in several degrees of leanness. When you are at the supermarket, know what you are buying. If a recipe calls for "lean ground beef," look for 80% to 85% lean. When the recipe calls for "extra-lean ground beef," go for 90% to 95% lean.

Italian Shepherd's Pie

Italian Shepherd's Pie

The mashed potatoes-and-cheese topper makes this beef, sausage, and veggie pie a satisfying dinner. Serve it with fresh fruit for dessert and your meal is complete.

PER SERVING: 224 cal., 8 g total fat (4 g sat. fat), 42 mg chol., 641 mg sodium, 22 g carb., 4 g fiber, 18 g pro. Exchanges: 1 vegetable, 1 starch, 2 lean meat. Carb choices: 1.5.

- **¾ cup shredded reduced-fat Italian-blend cheeses or reduced-fat mozzarella cheese (3 ounces)**
- **2 cups refrigerated mashed potatoes**
- **8 ounces 90% or higher lean ground beef**
- **4 ounces uncooked Italian turkey sausage links, casings removed**
- **½ cup chopped onion**
- **2 cups sliced zucchini or yellow summer squash**
- **1 14.5-ounce can diced tomatoes, undrained**
- **½ of a 6-ounce can (⅓ cup) tomato paste**
- **¼ teaspoon ground black pepper**
- **Paprika (optional)**

1. Preheat oven to 375°F. In a medium bowl, stir ½ cup of the cheese into potatoes; set mixture aside.

2. In a large skillet, combine ground beef, sausage, and onion; cook until meat is brown and onion is tender. Drain off fat. Stir zucchini, undrained tomatoes, tomato paste, and pepper into meat mixture in skillet. Bring to boiling.

3. Divide meat mixture among six 10-ounce individual casserole dishes or ramekins. Spoon mashed potato mixture into mounds on top of hot meat mixture in dishes. Sprinkle with remaining ¼ cup cheese. If desired, sprinkle with paprika.

4. Place dishes in a 15×10×1-inch baking pan. Bake, uncovered, for 25 minutes or until hot and bubbly. Let stand for 15 minutes before serving. **Makes 6 servings.**

Baked Ratatouille-Sausage Penne

In the mood for Italian? Try this low-fat sausage-and-eggplant one-dish pasta meal.

PER SERVING: 251 cal., 8 g total fat (2 g sat. fat), 39 mg chol., 559 mg sodium, 30 g carb., 6 g fiber, 17 g pro. Exchanges: 1 vegetable, 1.5 starch, 1.5 medium-fat meat. Carb choices: 2.

- **3 uncooked Italian turkey sausage links (12 ounces total)**
- **4 cloves garlic, minced**

Baked Ratatouille-Sausage Penne

- **1 teaspoon olive oil**
- **1 14.5-ounce can no-salt-added diced tomatoes**
- **3 tablespoons snipped fresh parsley**
- **¼ teaspoon crushed red pepper (optional)**
- **1 pound eggplant, peeled and cut into ½-inch cubes**
- **6 ounces dried whole wheat penne pasta (about 2¼ cups)**
- **⅓ cup finely shredded Parmesan cheese**
- **Snipped fresh parsley (optional)**

1. Preheat oven to 350°F. Place sausage links in an unheated skillet. Add ½ inch of water to the skillet. Bring to boiling; reduce heat. Cover and simmer about 15 minutes or until juices run clear; drain off liquid. Cook for 2 to 4 minutes more or until brown, turning occasionally. Remove from heat. When cool enough to handle, cut sausages in half lengthwise; bias-cut into ½-inch-thick slices. Set aside.

2. In a large skillet, cook garlic in hot olive oil for 1 minute. Stir in *undrained* tomatoes, the 3 tablespoons parsley, and, if desired, the crushed red pepper. Bring to boiling. Stir in eggplant; reduce heat. Cover and simmer for 15 minutes.

3. Meanwhile, cook pasta according to package directions, cooking it for the minimum time listed; drain. Return pasta to hot pan. Stir in eggplant mixture and sausage. Spoon into a 2-quart baking dish.

4. Cover with foil. Bake about 30 minutes or until heated through. Sprinkle with Parmesan cheese. Bake, uncovered, about 5 minutes more or until cheese melts. If desired, sprinkle with additional parsley. **Makes 6 (1 plus-cup) servings.**

(a fresh snip)

Fresh herbs do not require long cooking times to release the flavors like dried herbs do. To snip herbs with delicate stems, such as parsley, cilantro, basil, and mint, place the herbs, stems and all, in a small bowl or glass measuring cup. Then use a pair of clean kitchen shears to snip the herbs right in the container. Herbs with woody stems, such as thyme, oregano, and particularly rosemary, should be stripped from their stems before you use them. To do this, hold the stem in one hand, start at the top, and strip off the leaves by running the fingers of your other hand firmly down the stem. Snip the leaves as you would delicate herbs. Add near the end of cooking or to the finished dish.

Chicken Breasts with Red Pepper Sauce

Chicken Breasts with Red Pepper Sauce

Pureed red peppers make a fantastic low-calorie, low-carb sauce for this pasta, chicken, and green bean combo.

PER SERVING: 242 cal., 5 g total fat (1 g sat. fat), 53 mg chol., 323 mg sodium, 25 g carb., 5 g fiber, 26 g pro. Exchanges: 1.5 vegetable, 1 starch, 3 very lean meat, 0.5 fat. Carb choices: 1.5.

2 medium red sweet peppers, quartered, seeded, and stems and ribs removed
1 tablespoon olive oil
½ teaspoon salt
¼ to ½ teaspoon bottled hot pepper sauce
1 teaspoon Cajun seasoning
4 skinless, boneless chicken breast halves 1 to 1¼ pounds total)
4 ounces dried whole wheat linguine or fettuccine
3 cups fresh green beans (about 10 ounces), trimmed and bias-sliced into 1-inch pieces
Snipped fresh flat-leaf parsley

1. For red pepper sauce, place a steamer insert in a large skillet or 4-quart Dutch oven with a tight-fitting lid. Add water to skillet or Dutch oven to just below the steamer insert. Bring water to boiling. Place pepper quarters in the steamer insert. Cover and steam over medium heat about 18 minutes or until peppers are tender, adding more water as needed to maintain steam. Transfer pepper halves to a blender or food processor. Add olive oil, salt, and hot pepper sauce. Cover and blend or process until smooth. Set aside.

2. Sprinkle Cajun seasoning onto chicken. Place chicken in the steamer insert, overlapping thinner portions as needed. Cover and steam for 15 to 20 minutes or until chicken is tender and no longer pink (170°F), adding more water as needed to maintain steam.

3. Meanwhile, in a large saucepan, cook pasta according to package directions, adding green beans for the last

8 minutes of cooking. Drain and return to saucepan. Cut cooked chicken into bite-size pieces. Add chicken and red pepper sauce to pasta mixture. Toss to coat. Sprinkle with parsley. **Makes 5 (1¼-cup) servings.**

Apple-Glazed Chicken with Spinach

Apple jelly creates a glistening glaze.

PER SERVING: 268 cal., 2 g total fat (0 g sat. fat), 66 mg chol., 588 mg sodium, 35 g carb., 4 g fiber, 30 g pro. Exchanges: 2 vegetable, 0.5 fruit, 1 carb., 3.5 very lean meat. Carb choices: 2.

- **⅓ cup apple jelly**
- **2 tablespoons reduced-sodium soy sauce**
- **1 tablespoon snipped fresh thyme or 1 teaspoon dried thyme, crushed**
- **1 teaspoon finely shredded lemon peel**
- **1 teaspoon grated fresh ginger or ¼ teaspoon ground ginger**
- **4 skinless, boneless chicken breast halves (1 to 1¼ pounds total)**
- **¼ teaspoon salt**
- **¼ teaspoon ground black pepper**
- **Nonstick cooking spray**
- **2 medium apples, cored and coarsely chopped**
- **½ cup sliced onion**
- **2 cloves garlic, minced**
- **12 cups packaged fresh baby spinach**

1. Preheat broiler. For glaze, in a small microwave-safe bowl, combine apple jelly, soy sauce, thyme, lemon peel, and ginger. Microwave, uncovered, on 100% power (high) for 1 to 1¼ minutes or just until jelly is melted, stirring once. Set aside ¼ cup of the glaze.

2. Season chicken with ⅛ teaspoon of the salt and ⅛ teaspoon of the pepper. Place chicken on the unheated rack of a broiler pan. Broil 4 to 5 inches from heat for 12 to 15 minutes or until chicken is tender and no longer pink (170°F), turning once and brushing with the remaining glaze during the last 5 minutes of broiling.

3. Meanwhile, lightly coat an unheated large saucepan with nonstick cooking spray. Preheat over medium heat. Add apples, onion, and garlic; cook and stir for 3 minutes. Stir in the reserved ¼ cup glaze; bring to boiling. Add spinach; toss just until wilted. Sprinkle with the remaining ⅛ teaspoon salt and remaining ⅛ teaspoon pepper.

4. Serve chicken with spinach mixture. **Makes 4 servings.**

Apple-Glazed Chicken with Spinach

Balsamic-Dijon Chicken

Experiment with various flavored mustards.

PER SERVING: 161 cal., 1 g total fat (0 g sat. fat), 66 mg chol., 537 mg sodium, 3 g carb., 0 g fiber, 26 g pro. Exchanges: 4 very lean meat. Carb choices: 0.

- **4 skinless, boneless chicken breast halves (1 to 1¼ pounds total)**
- **⅓ cup Dijon-style mustard**
- **3 tablespoons balsamic vinegar**
- **2 cloves garlic, minced**
- **2 teaspoons snipped fresh thyme or basil or ½ teaspoon dried thyme or basil, crushed**
- **Fresh thyme sprigs (optional)**

1. Place chicken in a large resealable plastic bag in a shallow dish; set aside.

2. For marinade, in a small bowl, combine mustard, balsamic vinegar, garlic, and the snipped or dried thyme until well mixed. Pour marinade over chicken in bag. Seal bag; turn to coat chicken. Marinate in the refrigerator for 4 to 24 hours, turning bag occasionally.

3. Drain the chicken, reserving marinade. For a charcoal grill, place chicken on the grill rack directly over medium coals. Grill, uncovered, for 7 minutes, brushing occasionally with reserved marinade. Turn chicken; brush again with marinade. Discard any remaining marinade. Grill for 5 to 8 minutes more or until chicken is tender and no longer pink (170°F). (For a gas grill, preheat grill. Reduce heat to medium. Place chicken on grill rack over heat. Cover and grill as above.) If desired, garnish with thyme sprigs. **Makes 4 servings.**

Apricot Chicken Kabobs

Apricot spreadable fruit and jerk seasoning team up to give these chicken skewers a tantalizing zing. Another time, try strawberry spreadable fruit instead.

PER SERVING: 199 cal., 2 g total fat (0 g sat. fat), 66 mg chol., 173 mg sodium, 20 g carb., 2 g fiber, 27 g pro. Exchanges: 0.5 vegetable, 1 carb., 3.5 very lean meat. Carb choices: 1.

- **1 pound skinless, boneless chicken breast halves, cut into 1-inch pieces**
- **1½ teaspoons Jamaican jerk seasoning**
- **1 cup fresh sugar snap peas or snow pea pods, strings and tips removed**
- **1 cup fresh or canned pineapple cubes**
- **1 medium red sweet pepper, seeded and cut into 1-inch pieces**
- **¼ cup apricot spreadable fruit**

1. Place chicken in a large bowl. Sprinkle chicken with about half of the jerk seasoning; toss gently to coat. Cut any large pea pods in half crosswise.

2. Thread chicken, sugar snap peas, pineapple, and sweet pepper alternately on skewers,* leaving a ¼-inch space between pieces.

3. For sauce, in a small saucepan, combine remaining jerk seasoning and the spreadable fruit. Cook and stir just until spreadable fruit melts; set aside.

4. For a charcoal grill, place kabobs on the grill rack directly over medium coals. Grill, uncovered, for 8 to 12 minutes or until chicken is no longer pink and vegetables are crisp-tender, turning once and brushing occasionally with sauce during the last 3 minutes of grilling. (For a gas grill, preheat grill. Reduce heat to medium. Place kabobs on grill rack. Cover and grill as above.) **Makes 4 servings.**

***Test Kitchen Tip:** If using wooden skewers, soak in enough water to cover for at least 30 minutes before using.

Chicken Nuggets

Easy to make—by the time the oven preheats, the coated chicken chunks can be ready to bake.

PER SERVING: 191 cal., 2 g total fat (0 g sat. fat), 66 mg chol., 228 mg sodium, 13 g carb., 0 g fiber, 29 g pro. Exchanges: 1 starch, 3.5 very lean meat. Carb choices: 0.

- **⅔ cup crushed cornflakes**
- **1 teaspoon paprika**
- **½ teaspoon garlic powder**
- **½ teaspoon dried oregano, crushed**
- **⅛ teaspoon cayenne pepper (optional)**
- **1 egg white**
- **1 pound skinless, boneless chicken breast halves, cut into 1-inch pieces**

1. Preheat oven to 450°F. In a resealable plastic bag, combine crushed cornflakes, paprika, garlic powder, oregano, and, if desired, cayenne pepper. In a small bowl, beat egg white with a fork.

2. Dip chicken pieces into egg white, allowing excess to drain off. Add chicken pieces, a few at a time, to cornflake mixture in bag; shake to coat well.

3. Place chicken pieces in a single layer in an ungreased shallow baking pan. Bake for 7 to 9 minutes or until chicken is no longer pink. **Makes 4 servings.**

Quick Tip:

Let's face it, kids of all ages like to dip and dunk. Although these crisp-coated chicken chunks are quite tasty on their own, flavored mustard; low-carb, low-calorie ketchup; or low-carb, low-sodium pasta sauce makes healthful dippers.

Chicken Nuggets

Basil-Tomato Chicken Skillet

If chicken breast tenderloins are not available, cut skinless, boneless chicken breast halves lengthwise into thirds.

PER SERVING: 170 cal., 2 g total fat (1 g sat. fat), 68 mg chol., 265 mg sodium, 7 g carb., 3 g fiber, 30 g pro. Exchanges: 1.5 vegetable, 4 very lean meat. Carb choices: 0.5.

- **1 to 1¼ pounds chicken breast tenderloins**
- **Nonstick cooking spray**
- **⅛ teaspoon salt**
- **⅛ teaspoon ground black pepper**
- **1 14.5-ounce can no-salt-added diced tomatoes, drained**
- **¼ cup snipped fresh basil**
- **1 9- to 10-ounce package prewashed fresh spinach**
- **2 tablespoons finely shredded Parmesan cheese**

1. Cut any large chicken tenderloins in half lengthwise. Coat an unheated very large skillet with nonstick cooking spray. Heat over medium-high heat.

2. Cook and stir chicken in hot skillet about 5 minutes or until no longer pink. Sprinkle with salt and pepper.

3. Add tomatoes and basil; heat through. Remove from heat. Add spinach; toss until wilted. Divide among four serving plates. Sprinkle with cheese. **Makes 4 (about 2-cup) servings.**

Basil-Tomato Chicken Skillet

Cashew Chicken

A handy pouch of rice saves prep time, but you can cook your own brown rice if you prefer.

PER SERVING: 362 cal., 11 g total fat (2 g sat. fat), 66 mg chol., 436 mg sodium, 32 g carb., 2 g fiber, 32 g pro. Exchanges: 1 vegetable, 1.5 starch, 4 lean meat, 1 fat. Carb choices: 2.

¼ cup reduced-sodium teriyaki sauce
2 teaspoons cornstarch
2 cloves garlic, minced
¼ to ½ teaspoon crushed red pepper
⅓ cup water
1 tablespoon canola oil
1 16-ounce package frozen stir-fry vegetable blend
1 pound packaged chicken stir-fry strips
1 8.8-ounce pouch cooked whole grain brown rice
¼ cup lightly salted roasted cashews, coarsely chopped
1 green onion, thinly sliced
Salt (optional)

1. For sauce, in a small bowl, whisk together teriyaki sauce, cornstarch, garlic, and crushed red pepper until well combined. Whisk in the water. Set aside.

2. In a large wok or a very large nonstick skillet, heat oil over medium-high heat. Add stir-fry vegetables; stir-fry for 5 to 6 minutes or until vegetables are crisp-tender. Remove vegetables from wok and set aside.

3. Add chicken to wok. Stir-fry for 3 to 4 minutes or until chicken is no longer pink (if necessary, add 1 teaspoon additional canola oil). Push chicken to the side of wok. Stir sauce; add to wok. Cook and stir until thickened and bubbly. Return vegetable mixture to wok. Cook and stir about 1 minute more or until heated through.

4. Meanwhile, heat rice according to package directions. Divide rice among four serving plates. Top with chicken mixture, cashews, and green onion. If desired, season to taste with salt. **Makes 4 servings (⅓ cup rice with 1 cup chicken mixture per serving).**

Tortilla-Crusted Chicken

Tortilla-Crusted Chicken

Place the tortilla chips in a resealable plastic bag and use your hand to crush them.

PER SERVING: 230 cal., 6 g total fat (1 g sat. fat), 135 mg chol., 143 mg sodium, 7 g carb., 1 g fiber, 35 g pro. Exchanges: 0.5 starch, 4.5 very lean meat, 1 fat. Carb choices: 0.

Nonstick cooking spray
1 cup finely crushed multigrain tortilla chips
½ teaspoon dried oregano, crushed
¼ teaspoon ground cumin
¼ teaspoon freshly ground black pepper
1 egg
4 skinless, boneless chicken breast halves (about 1¼ pounds total)
Shredded romaine lettuce (optional)
Purchased salsa (optional)
Avocado slices (optional)

1. Preheat oven to 375°F. Coat a 15×10×1-inch baking pan with nonstick cooking spray; set aside. In a shallow dish, combine tortilla chips, oregano, cumin, and pepper. In another shallow dish, beat egg lightly with a fork. Dip chicken in beaten egg, then roll it in the tortilla chip mixture to coat.

2. Arrange chicken in the prepared baking pan. Bake about 25 minutes or until chicken is no longer pink (170°F). If desired, serve chicken on a bed of shredded romaine with salsa and avocado slices. **Makes 4 servings.**

Creamy Chicken Enchiladas

Creamy Chicken Enchiladas

Accompany this spicy dish with a cool salad of mixed greens embellished with tomato wedges and tossed with a reduced-fat dressing.

PER SERVING: 269 cal., 11 g total fat (6 g sat. fat), 47 mg chol., 618 mg sodium, 24 g carb., 2 g fiber, 20 g pro. Exchanges: 1 vegetable, 1 starch, 2 lean meat, 1 fat. Carb choices: 1.5.

8 ounces skinless, boneless chicken breast halves
⅔ cup water
¼ teaspoon ground black pepper
1 10-ounce package frozen chopped spinach, thawed and well drained
2 tablespoons thinly sliced green onion
1 8-ounce tub light cream cheese
2 tablespoons all-purpose flour
¼ teaspoon ground cumin
¼ cup fat-free milk
1 4-ounce can diced green chiles, drained
Nonstick cooking spray
6 7-inch white or whole wheat flour tortillas
½ cup bottled salsa
½ cup shredded reduced-fat cheddar or Monterey Jack cheese (2 ounces)
Chopped romaine lettuce (optional)
Thinly sliced green onions (optional)
Snipped fresh cilantro (optional)

1. Preheat oven to 350°F. In a large skillet, combine chicken, the water, and black pepper. Bring to boiling; reduce heat. Cover and simmer for 12 to 14 minutes or until chicken is no longer pink. Drain well; cool slightly. When cool enough to handle, use two forks to shred chicken into bite-size pieces; set aside.

2. For filling, in a large bowl, combine shredded chicken, spinach, and the 2 tablespoons green onion. In a small bowl, combine cream cheese, flour, and cumin. Stir in milk and chiles. Stir the cheese mixture into the chicken mixture.

3. Coat a 2-quart rectangular baking dish with nonstick cooking spray. Divide the filling among the tortillas. Roll up tortillas. Place tortillas, seam sides up, in the prepared dish.

4. Cover dish with foil. Bake for 20 minutes. Pour salsa over enchiladas and sprinkle with cheese. Bake, uncovered, about 20 minutes more or until heated through and cheese melts. Let stand for 5 minutes before serving. If desired, sprinkle with lettuce, additional green onions, and cilantro. **Makes 6 servings.**

Chicken Tostadas with Black Bean Salsa

Before juicing the lime, roll it on the countertop a few times to help break the juice cells and release the juices.

PER SERVING: 206 cal., 2 g total fat (0 g sat. fat), 39 mg chol., 285 mg sodium, 28 g carb., 6 g fiber, 23 g pro. Exchanges: 0.5 vegetable, 1.5 starch, 2.5 very lean meat. Carb choices: 2.

6 6-inch corn tortillas
Nonstick cooking spray
1 14-ounce can reduced-sodium chicken broth
1 teaspoon chili powder
1 teaspoon ground cumin
½ teaspoon dried oregano, crushed
3 skinless, boneless chicken breast halves (14 to 16 ounces total)
1 15-ounce can black beans, rinsed and drained
¾ cup frozen whole kernel corn, thawed
½ cup chopped fresh tomato
¼ cup chopped onion
¼ cup snipped fresh cilantro
3 tablespoons lime juice
⅛ teaspoon ground black pepper
2 cups shredded romaine lettuce
Fresh cilantro sprigs (optional)
⅓ cup light dairy sour cream (optional)
Lime wedges (optional)

1. Preheat oven to 400°F. Coat both sides of tortillas with nonstick cooking spray. Place on baking sheets. Bake for 7 to 9 minutes or until lightly browned. Transfer to wire racks to cool. Tortillas will crisp as they cool.

2. Meanwhile, in a large skillet, combine broth, chili powder, cumin, and oregano. Bring to boiling; add chicken. Return to boiling; reduce heat. Cover and simmer for 8 to 10 minutes or until chicken is no longer pink (170°F). Remove from heat. Let chicken cool in the liquid about 15 minutes or until cool enough to handle. Transfer chicken to a cutting board. Use two forks to shred chicken into large pieces. Return shredded chicken to the cooking liquid.

3. In a medium bowl, combine beans, corn, tomato, onion, snipped cilantro, lime juice, and pepper.

4. Place tortillas on serving plates. Top with lettuce and bean mixture. Using a slotted spoon, spoon chicken over bean mixture. If desired, garnish with cilantro sprigs and serve with sour cream and lime wedges. **Makes 6 servings.**

Baked Herb Salmon

Baked Herb Salmon

Carefully check over the salmon, removing all bones before you sprinkle on the herbs and seasonings.

PER SERVING: 184 cal., 11 g total fat (2 g sat. fat), 58 mg chol., 132 mg sodium, 2 g carb., 1 g fiber, 20 g pro. Exchanges: 3 lean meat. Carb choices: 0.

1 2-pound fresh or frozen salmon fillet (with skin)
1 tablespoon snipped fresh chives
1 tablespoon snipped fresh thyme or 1 teaspoon dried thyme, crushed
½ teaspoon ground black pepper
¼ teaspoon salt
1 lemon, cut into ⅛-inch slices and seeded

1. Thaw fish, if frozen. Line a large baking sheet with foil. Preheat oven to 400° F. Rinse fish; pat dry with paper towels. Place salmon, skin side down, on the foil-lined baking sheet. Sprinkle salmon with chives, thyme, pepper, and salt. Top with lemon slices.

2. Cover salmon with foil. Bake for 20 minutes. Uncover and bake for 20 to 25 minutes more or until salmon flakes easily when tested with a fork. Serve immediately. **Makes 8 servings.**

Grilled Salmon with Citrus Salsa

Although the refreshing orange-and-pineapple salsa is teamed with salmon in this recipe, it also makes a terrific topper for most other types of fish as well as grilled chicken.

PER SERVING: 253 cal., 12 g total fat (2 g sat. fat), 66 mg chol., 457 mg sodium, 11 g carb., 2 g fiber, 23 g pro. Exchanges: 0.5 fruit, 3.5 lean meat, 0.5 fat. Carb choices: 1.

1 1½-pound fresh or frozen salmon fillet (with skin), 1 inch thick
1 tablespoon sugar
1½ teaspoons finely shredded orange peel
1 teaspoon salt
¼ teaspoon freshly ground black pepper
Nonstick cooking spray
1 recipe Citrus Salsa (see recipe, below)

1. Thaw fish, if frozen. Rinse fish; pat dry with paper towels. Cut into 6 serving-size portions. In a small bowl, stir together sugar, orange peel, salt, and pepper. Sprinkle sugar mixture evenly onto skinless sides of salmon. Place salmon, sugar sides up, in a glass baking dish. Cover and chill for 8 to 24 hours.

2. Coat an unheated grill rack with nonstick cooking spray. For a charcoal grill, arrange medium-hot coals around a drip pan. Test for medium heat above drip pan. Drain salmon, discarding liquid. Place salmon pieces, skin sides down, on the grill rack over the drip pan. Cover and grill for 14 to 18 minutes or until fish flakes easily when tested with a fork. (For a gas grill, preheat grill. Reduce heat to medium. Adjust for indirect cooking. Grill as above.)

3. If desired, carefully slip a metal spatula between fish and skin; lift fish up and away from skin; discard skin. Serve fish with Citrus Salsa. **Makes 6 servings (1 piece of fish with ⅓ cup salsa per serving).**

Citrus Salsa: In a small bowl, combine 1 teaspoon finely shredded orange peel; 2 oranges, peeled, sectioned, and chopped; 1 cup chopped fresh pineapple or canned pineapple tidbits (juice pack), drained; 2 tablespoons snipped fresh cilantro; 1 sliced green onion; and 1 fresh jalapeño pepper, seeded and finely chopped.* Cover and chill until ready to serve or up to 24 hours.

***Test Kitchen Tip:** Because chile peppers contain volatile oils that can burn your skin and eyes, avoid direct contact with them as much as possible. When working with chile peppers, wear plastic or rubber gloves. If your bare hands do touch the peppers, wash your hands and nails well with soap and warm water.

(perfectly cooked)

Cooking fish too long causes it to become tough and dry. Follow these simple steps for moist and tender fish. As a general rule, it takes 4 to 6 minutes of cooking per ½-inch thickness of fish. Check the doneness of the fish at the thickest part of the fillet. When the fish is cooked, it will be opaque, moist, and pull apart easily when tested with a fork. For thicker, denser fish steaks where the fork test is difficult, insert an instant-read thermometer horizontally into the steak. When the internal temperature of the fish steak is 140°F, the fish is done.

Cod Amandine

Cod Amandine

Baking in a hot oven, rather than frying, turns these crumb-coated cod fillets crispy and golden.

PER SERVING: 191 cal., 7 g total fat (1 g sat. fat), 49 mg chol., 245 mg sodium, 7 g carb., 1 g fiber, 23 g pro. Exchanges: 0.5 starch, 3 very lean meat, 1 fat. Carb choices: 0.5.

4 4-ounce fresh or frozen skinless cod, tilapia, trout, or halibut fillets, ½ to 1 inch thick
¼ cup buttermilk
½ cup panko (Japanese-style) bread crumbs or fine dry bread crumbs
2 tablespoons snipped fresh parsley or 2 teaspoons dried parsley flakes
½ teaspoon dry mustard
¼ teaspoon salt
⅛ teaspoon ground black pepper
¼ cup sliced almonds, coarsely chopped
1 tablespoon olive oil
Lemon wedges (optional)

1. Thaw fish, if frozen. Grease a shallow baking pan; set aside. Preheat oven to 450°F. Rinse fish; pat dry with paper towels. Measure thickness of fish.

2. Pour buttermilk into a shallow dish. In another shallow dish, combine bread crumbs, parsley, dry mustard, salt, and pepper. Dip fish into buttermilk, then coat fish with crumb mixture. Place coated fish in prepared baking pan.

3. Sprinkle fish with almonds. Drizzle olive oil over fish. Bake for 4 to 6 minutes per ½-inch thickness of fish or until fish flakes easily when tested with a fork. Serve fish with lemon wedges, if desired. **Makes 4 servings.**

Broiled Tuna Fajitas

Ancho and Lime Seared Scallops

Broiled Tuna Fajitas

Extra salsa? Serve it on scrambled eggs, drizzle it over salad greens, or spoon it into baked scoop-shape tortilla chips.

PER SERVING: 285 cal., 9 g total fat (2 g sat. fat), 27 mg chol., 440 mg sodium, 33 g carb., 6 g fiber, 21 g pro. Exchanges: 1 vegetable, 2 starch, 2 very lean meat, 1 fat. Carb choices: 0.

2 5- to 6-ounce fresh or frozen tuna or halibut steaks, cut 1 inch thick
¼ cup lime juice
2 tablespoons snipped fresh cilantro or parsley
1 tablespoon olive oil
2 cloves garlic, minced
¼ teaspoon coarsely ground black pepper
⅛ teaspoon cayenne pepper
8 6-inch corn tortillas
Nonstick cooking spray
2 medium red and/or yellow sweet peppers, quartered and stems and membranes removed
1 cup purchased tomato salsa or tomatillo salsa

1. Thaw fish, if frozen. Rinse fish; pat dry with paper towels. Place fish in a large resealable plastic bag set in a shallow dish.

2. For marinade, in a small bowl, stir together lime juice, cilantro, oil, garlic, black pepper, and cayenne pepper. Pour marinade over fish in bag. Seal bag; turn to coat fish. Marinate in the refrigerator for 30 minutes, turning bag occasionally.

3. Preheat broiler. Wrap tortillas tightly in foil. Drain fish, reserving marinade. Lightly coat the unheated rack of a broiler pan with nonstick cooking spray. Place fish on prepared broiler pan. Place sweet pepper quarters beside fish. Place wrapped tortillas alongside the broiler pan. Broil fish 4 to 5 inches from heat for 8 to 12 minutes or just until fish flakes easily when tested with a fork, brushing once with reserved marinade after 3 minutes of broiling and turning once halfway through broiling. Discard any remaining marinade. Broil sweet peppers about 8 minutes or until tender, turning occasionally. Broil tortillas about 8 minutes or until heated through, turning once.

4. Using a fork, break fish into large chunks. Cut sweet peppers into ½-inch-wide strips. Immediately fill warm tortillas with fish and sweet pepper strips. Serve with salsa. **Makes 4 servings.**

Ancho and Lime Seared Scallops

Jump-start the meal by making the salsa the night before.

PER SERVING: 188 cal., 1 g total fat (0 g sat. fat), 47 mg chol., 333 mg sodium, 19 g carb., 2 g fiber, 25 g pro. Exchanges: 1 fruit, 3.5 very lean meat. Carb choices: 1.

12 fresh or frozen sea scallops (1¼ to 1½ pounds total)
½ teaspoon ancho chili powder or regular chili powder
⅛ teaspoon salt
Nonstick cooking spray
1 tablespoon lime juice
1 recipe Tropical Fruit Salsa (see recipe, below)

1. Thaw scallops, if frozen. Rinse scallops; pat dry with paper towels. In a small bowl, combine chili powder and salt. Sprinkle chili powder mixture evenly over scallops; rub in with your fingers.

2. Lightly coat an unheated large nonstick skillet with nonstick cooking spray. Preheat over medium-high heat. Add scallops to hot skillet. Cook for 4 to 6 minutes or until opaque, turning once. Transfer scallops to a serving plate. Drizzle with lime juice; cover to keep warm.

3. Add Tropical Fruit Salsa to skillet. Cook and stir about 1 minute or until heated through, scraping up the brown bits from bottom of skillet. Serve warmed salsa with the scallops. **Makes 4 servings (3 scallops with ½ cup salsa per serving).**

Tropical Fruit Salsa: In a medium bowl, combine 1 tablespoon snipped fresh mint, 2 teaspoons seasoned rice vinegar, 2 teaspoons lime juice, ½ to 1 teaspoon grated fresh ginger or ¼ teaspoon ground ginger, and, if desired, ⅛ teaspoon crushed red pepper. Add ½ cup chopped fresh pineapple, ½ cup chopped mango or peach, ½ cup chopped peeled kiwifruit, and one 5-ounce container mandarin orange sections, drained; toss gently to coat. Serve immediately or cover and chill for up to 24 hours.

Cajun Shrimp with Mango-Edamame Salsa

Cajun Shrimp with Mango-Edamame Salsa

Stir up our homemade Cajun seasoning if you can't find salt-free seasoning mix for the shrimp.

PER SERVING: 317 cal., 12 g total fat (2 g sat. fat), 129 mg chol., 287 mg sodium, 29 g carb., 6 g fiber, 27 g pro. Exchanges: 0.5 vegetable, 0.5 fruit, 1 starch, 3.5 very lean meat, 1.5 fat. Carb choices: 1.5.

1 pound fresh or frozen large shrimp with tails
2 teaspoons purchased salt-free Cajun seasoning or Cajun Seasoning (see recipe, below)
1 tablespoon soybean cooking oil
1 recipe Mango-Edamame Salsa (see recipe, below)
Belgian endive leaves (optional)

1. Thaw shrimp, if frozen. Peel and devein shrimp, leaving tails intact if desired. Rinse shrimp; pat dry with paper towels. Set aside.

2. In a bowl, toss shrimp with Cajun seasoning. In a large skillet, heat oil over medium-high heat. Add shrimp; cook and stir for 5 minutes or until shrimp are pink.

3. Serve shrimp warm with Mango-Edamame Salsa and, if desired, Belgian endive leaves. **Makes 4 servings (about 5 shrimp with 3/4 cup salsa per serving).**

Cajun Seasoning: In a bowl, combine 1/2 teaspoon onion powder, 1/2 teaspoon paprika, 1/4 teaspoon ground white pepper, 1/4 teaspoon garlic powder, 1/4 teaspoon cayenne pepper, and 1/4 teaspoon ground black pepper.

Mango-Edamame Salsa: In a medium bowl, combine 2 seeded, peeled, and chopped mangoes; 1 cup fresh or frozen shelled sweet soybeans (edamame), cooked and cooled; 3/4 cup chopped red sweet pepper; 1/2 cup finely chopped green onions; 1/4 cup snipped fresh cilantro; 2 teaspoons soybean cooking oil; and 1/4 teaspoon salt. Toss gently to mix. Cover and chill until serving time or up to 2 hours.

Shrimp-Zucchini Kabobs with Basil Cream Sauce

If using wooden skewers, soak them in enough water to cover for 30 minutes before using and then drain.

PER SERVING: 185 cal., 10 g total fat (3 g sat. fat), 121 mg chol., 434 mg sodium, 7 g carb., 1 g fiber, 17 g pro. Exchanges: 1.5 vegetable, 2.5 very lean meat, 1.5 fat. Carb choices: 0.5.

1 8-ounce container light dairy sour cream
1/2 cup snipped fresh basil
3 tablespoons snipped fresh chives
3/4 teaspoon salt
1/8 teaspoon ground black pepper
1 1/4 pounds fresh or frozen large shrimp
2 medium zucchini, halved lengthwise and cut into 1-inch-thick slices (about 1 pound total)
2 tablespoons olive oil
1/2 teaspoon finely shredded orange peel or lime peel
1 tablespoon orange juice or lime juice
1/4 teaspoon cayenne pepper
5 cups fresh arugula and/or baby spinach

1. For sauce, in a food processor or blender, combine sour cream, basil, chives, 1/2 teaspoon of the salt, and the black pepper. Process or blend until nearly smooth. Cover and chill until ready to serve.

2. Thaw shrimp, if frozen. Peel and devein shrimp, leaving tails intact. Rinse shrimp; pat dry with paper towels. On long skewers, alternately thread shrimp and zucchini, leaving a 1/4-inch space between pieces. In a bowl, combine oil, orange peel, orange juice, cayenne pepper, and the remaining 1/4 teaspoon salt; brush evenly on shrimp and zucchini.

3. For a charcoal grill, place kabobs on the greased grill rack directly over medium coals. Grill, uncovered, about 10 minutes or until shrimp are opaque, turning once. (For a gas grill, preheat grill. Reduce heat to medium. Place kabobs on the grill rack over heat. Cover and grill as above.)

4. Arrange arugula on a platter; add kabobs. Serve sauce with skewers. **Makes 6 servings.**

(eating by the sea)

A traditional Mediterranean diet including foods that are naturally rich in antioxidants, fiber, and other nutrients has been linked to a lower risk of chronic diseases. Here are some of the main components.

1. **Plant foods,** including fruits, vegetables, whole grains, beans, nuts, and seeds, make up a large part of the diet.
2. **Fresh fruit** is the typical dessert; richer sweets are eaten occasionally.
3. **Minimally processed,** seasonally fresh, and locally grown foods are encouraged.
4. **Olive oil** is the main fat, replacing butter and margarine.
5. **Limited saturated fat** contributes no more than 7–8 percent of daily calories, or 16–18 grams on a 2,000-calorie diet.
6. **Cheese and yogurt** (low-fat and nonfat varieties) are eaten in small amounts daily.
7. **Fish, poultry, and eggs** are eaten weekly rather than daily, with an emphasis on fish.
8. **Red meat** is eaten only occasionally and the cuts are lean (12–16 ounces total each month).
9. **Wine** is consumed in moderation with meals (one glass a day for women and no more than two glasses a day for men), except during pregnancy or if it poses a health risk.
10. **Daily physical activity** is encouraged to promote a healthful weight, fitness, and well-being.

Shrimp-Zucchini Kabobs with Basil Cream Sauce

Fresh-Herb Pasta Primavera

Fresh-Herb Pasta Primavera

For lots of color, use a variety of veggies.

PER SERVING: 253 cal., 5 g total fat (3 g sat. fat), 12 mg chol., 496 mg sodium, 41 g carb., 6 g fiber, 13 g pro. Exchanges: 0.5 vegetable, 2.5 starch, 0.5 medium-fat meat. Carb choices: 3.

8 ounces dried multigrain or whole grain penne or mostaccioli
3 cups assorted fresh vegetables (such as red sweet pepper strips, trimmed sugar snap peas, 2-inch-long pieces trimmed asparagus, and/or quartered-lengthwise packaged peeled baby carrots)
1 cup halved cherry tomatoes
½ cup reduced-sodium chicken broth
3 tablespoons all-purpose flour
½ teaspoon salt
1¼ cups low-fat milk
¼ cup dry sherry or reduced-sodium chicken broth
¾ cup finely shredded Parmesan or Asiago cheese (3 ounces)
½ cup lightly packed fresh basil, coarsely chopped
4 teaspoons snipped fresh thyme or oregano
⅓ cup sliced green onions (optional)

1. In a 4-quart Dutch oven, cook pasta according to package directions, adding the 3 cups assorted vegetables for the last 2 minutes of cooking. Drain well. Return to hot Dutch oven. Add cherry tomatoes.

2. For sauce, in a medium saucepan, whisk together broth, flour, and salt until smooth. Stir in milk and sherry. Cook and stir until thickened and bubbly; cook and stir for 2 minutes more. Remove from heat; stir in Parmesan cheese, basil, and thyme.

3. Add sauce to pasta mixture; toss gently to coat. Divide among six serving plates. If desired, sprinkle with green onions. **Makes 6 (1⅓-cup) servings.**

Garden Vegetables Lasagna

Loads of veggies replace traditional meat sauce.

PER SERVING: 296 cal., 9 g total fat (5 g sat. fat), 41 mg chol., 426 mg sodium, 31 g carb., 6 g fiber, 20 g pro. Exchanges: 1 vegetable. 1.5 starch, 2 medium-fat meat. Carb choices: 2.

Nonstick cooking spray
9 dried whole grain or regular lasagna noodles
3 cups broccoli florets
2 red sweet peppers, seeded and cut into bite-size strips (2 cups)
2 medium yellow summer squash and/or zucchini, sliced (about 2½ cups)
2 15-ounce cartons light ricotta cheese
½ cup snipped fresh basil or 1 tablespoon dried basil, crushed
1 tablespoon snipped fresh thyme or 1 teaspoon dried thyme, crushed
3 cloves garlic, minced
½ teaspoon salt
¼ teaspoon ground black pepper
¼ teaspoon bottled hot pepper sauce
2 cups shredded reduced-fat mozzarella cheese (8 ounces)
¼ cup shredded fresh basil (optional)

1. Preheat oven to 375°F. Lightly coat a 3-quart rectangular baking dish with nonstick cooking spray; set aside. In a 4-quart Dutch oven, cook lasagna noodles in a large amount of boiling water for 10 to 12 minutes or until tender but still firm; drain. Rinse with cold water; drain again.

2. Place a steamer insert in the 4-quart Dutch oven. Add water to the Dutch oven to just below the steamer insert. Bring water to boiling. Place broccoli, sweet peppers, and squash in steamer insert. Cover and steam over medium heat for 6 to 8 minutes or until vegetables are crisp-tender. Remove from heat.

3. In a large bowl, combine ricotta cheese, ½ cup basil, the thyme, garlic, salt, black pepper, and hot pepper sauce. To assemble, layer three of the cooked noodles in the prepared baking dish. Spread with one-third of the ricotta cheese mixture. Top with one-third of the vegetable mixture and ⅔ cup of the mozzarella cheese. Repeat layers twice.

4. Cover dish with foil. Bake for 45 to 55 minutes or until heated through. Uncover and let stand for 10 minutes before serving. If desired, sprinkle with the ¼ cup basil. **Makes 8 servings.**

Garden Vegetables Lasagna

(surprise, it's squash)

The smooth, watermelon-shape yellow squash known as spaghetti squash is named for its strands of thin spaghetti-like flesh. To cook spaghetti squash, cut the squash lengthwise in half. Place one half, cut side down, in a microwave-safe baking dish. Using a fork, prick the skin all over. Microwave on 100% power (high) for 6 to 7 minutes or until tender when pierced with a fork; carefully remove from baking dish. Repeat with the other half. (Or place both halves, cut sides down, in a shallow baking pan. Bake in a 350°F oven for 30 to 40 minutes or until tender.) Cool slightly; using two forks, shred and separate squash pulp into strands.

Spaghetti Squash with Chunky Tomato Sauce

Spaghetti Squash with Chunky Tomato Sauce

Delicious served over the squash, this garden-fresh sauce is great spooned over polenta, too.

PER SERVING: 197 cal., 8 g total fat (3 g sat. fat), 10 mg chol., 588 mg sodium, 25 g carb., 6 g fiber, 9 g pro. Exchanges: 4 vegetable, 0.5 lean meat, 1.5 fat. Carb choices: 1.5.

1 tablespoon olive oil
1 cup coarsely chopped zucchini
⅔ cup chopped onion
½ cup shredded carrot
2 cloves garlic, minced
1 14.5-ounce can no-salt-added diced tomatoes, undrained
1 8-ounce can tomato sauce
2 tablespoons tomato paste
2 teaspoons dried Italian seasoning, crushed
⅛ teaspoon black pepper
4 cups cooked spaghetti squash (see tip, page 38)
¼ cup shredded Parmesan cheese (2 ounces)
Small fresh basil leaves (optional)

1. For chunky tomato sauce, in a large saucepan, heat oil over medium heat. Add zucchini, onion, carrot, and garlic; cook until tender, stirring occasionally. Add undrained diced tomatoes, tomato sauce, tomato paste, Italian seasoning, and pepper. Bring to boiling; reduce heat. Simmer, uncovered, for 15 minutes, stirring occasionally.

2. Serve chunky tomato sauce over spaghetti squash. Sprinkle with Parmesan cheese. If desired, garnish with basil leaves. **Makes 4 servings (1 cup sauce with 1 cup squash per serving).**

Vegetarian Tostada

Although it serves only two, this tasty recipe is easy to multiply and fun to serve a group. Set out bowls of the ingredients and let everyone make their own tostadas.

PER SERVING: 210 cal., 4 g total fat (1 g sat. fat), 4 mg chol., 438 mg sodium, 38 g carb., 8 g fiber, 8 g pro. Exchanges: 2 vegetable, 2 starch. Carb choices: 2.5.

⅔ cup cooked brown rice
⅔ cup canned pinto beans, black beans, or red beans, rinsed and drained
3 cups coarsely shredded mixed greens or fresh spinach
1 cup chopped tomato
¼ cup chopped onion
2 tablespoons shredded carrot
2 tablespoons sliced pitted ripe olives, halved
2 tablespoons purchased salsa
2 tablespoons light dairy sour cream
¼ of a medium avocado, peeled and sliced (optional)

1. Divide rice between two serving plates. Top with beans, greens, tomato, onion, carrot, olives, salsa, and sour cream. If desired, garnish with avocado slices. **Makes 2 servings.**

main-dish salads

Cranberry-Turkey Spinach Salad

When filled with fresh veggies and all the natural goodness that comes with them, a main-dish salad becomes a one-dish delight. Discover over a dozen fabulously flavorful, easy-to-assemble salad combos that help make eating more vegetables more enjoyable.

Cranberry-Turkey Spinach Salad

Cut the cranberry sauce into stars for Christmas or hearts for Valentine's Day.

PER SERVING: 120 cal., 1 g total fat (0 g sat. fat), 20 mg chol., 131 mg sodium, 17 g carb., 2 g fiber, 10 g pro. Exchanges: 2 vegetable, 0.5 carb., 1 very lean meat. Carb choices: 1.

1 8-ounce can or ½ of a 16-ounce can jellied cranberry sauce
⅓ cup cider vinegar
2 teaspoons coarsely snipped fresh sage or tarragon or ½ teaspoon dried leaf sage or dried tarragon, crushed
¼ teaspoon salt
⅛ teaspoon ground black pepper
12 cups packaged fresh baby spinach
8 ounces cooked turkey breast, thinly sliced, coarsely chopped, or shredded
1 medium cucumber, halved lengthwise, seeded if desired, and thinly sliced (about 2 cups)
6 ounces jicama, peeled and cut into thin bite-size strips (about 1½ cups)
6 medium radishes, thinly sliced
½ of a red onion, cut into thin wedges

1. Cut jellied cranberry sauce into ½-inch-thick slices. Using 1- to 1¼-inch cutters, cut 16 designs from the cranberry sauce slices; set aside.

2. For dressing, place remaining scraps of cranberry sauce in a blender; add vinegar, sage, salt, and pepper. Cover and blend until combined. Set aside.

3. In a large bowl, toss together spinach, turkey, cucumber, jicama, radishes, and red onion. Divide among eight serving bowls. Add two of the cranberry cutouts to each serving; drizzle with dressing. **Makes 8 (about 2 cup) servings.**

Quick Tip:

Whenever you have some extra chicken—from Friday's cookout or Sunday's roasted bird—place it in a freezer container and freeze for up to 3 months. A little bit of chicken left over from here and there can add up to the right amount for a quick chicken salad.

Lime Chicken on Cilantro Corn Salad

A little lime-laced marinade delivers a lot of flavor.

PER SERVING: 263 cal., 9 g total fat (1 g sat. fat), 55 mg chol., 259 mg sodium, 23 g carb., 3 g fiber, 25 g pro. Exchanges: 1.5 starch, 3 lean meat, 0.5 fat. Carb choices: 1.5.

- **1¼ pounds chicken breast tenderloins**
- **3 tablespoons olive oil**
- **1 teaspoon finely shredded lime peel**
- **2 tablespoons lime juice**
- **1 clove garlic, minced**
- **½ teaspoon salt**
- **¼ cup snipped fresh cilantro**
- **3 cups fresh or frozen whole kernel corn, cooked and chilled**
- **2 small tomatoes, cut into thin wedges**

1. Place chicken in a resealable plastic bag set in a shallow bowl; set aside. In a small bowl, whisk together oil, lime peel, lime juice, garlic, and salt. Stir in cilantro. Pour half of the lime mixture over chicken in bag. Seal bag; turn to coat. Marinate in the refrigerator for 1 to 2 hours, turning bag occasionally. Cover remaining lime mixture; set aside.

2. Preheat a very large skillet over medium-high heat. Add chicken mixture to hot skillet. Cook for 4 to 6 minutes or until chicken is no longer pink, turning occasionally.

3. Meanwhile, in a medium bowl, combine corn and tomatoes. Add reserved lime mixture, tossing until combined. Spoon corn mixture onto four serving plates. Top with cooked chicken. **Makes 6 servings.**

Chicken, Apple, and Bibb Lettuce Salad

Take your pick—red or green apples are equally delicious.

PER SERVING: 313 cal., 11 g total fat (2 g sat. fat), 89 mg chol., 227 mg sodium, 20 g carb., 2 g fiber, 33 g pro. Exchanges: 1 vegetable, 0.5 fruit, 0.5 carb., 4 lean meat, 1 fat. Carb choices: 1.

- **2 tablespoons champagne vinegar or white wine vinegar**
- **2 tablespoons olive oil**
- **2 tablespoons honey**
- **¼ teaspoon salt**
- **⅛ teaspoon ground black pepper**
- **1 head butterhead (Bibb or Boston) lettuce, trimmed and separated into leaves**
- **3 cups shredded cooked chicken breast**
- **2 medium apples, cored and sliced**
- **1 small shallot or 2 green onions, chopped**
- **Ground black pepper**

1. In a small bowl, whisk together vinegar, oil, honey, salt, and the ⅛ teaspoon pepper. Divide lettuce leaves among four serving plates. Top with chicken, apples, and shallot. Whisk dressing and drizzle over salads. Sprinkle with additional pepper. **Makes 4 servings.**

Chicken Salad with Peanut Dressing

Dress up leftover cooked chicken with fruit salad and a fabulous peanut butter, soy sauce, and ginger dressing.

PER SERVING: 209 cal., 7 g total fat (2 g sat. fat), 60 mg chol., 188 mg sodium, 12 g carb., 3 g fiber, 26 g pro. Exchanges: 1.5 vegetable, 0.5 fruit, 3 lean meat, 0.5 fat. Carb choices: 1.

- **6 cups coarsely torn napa cabbage or romaine lettuce**
- **2 cups coarsely shredded cooked chicken breast (about 10 ounces)**
- **1 small apple, cored and thinly sliced**
- **½ cup red and/or green seedless grapes, halved**
- **3 tablespoons water**
- **2 tablespoons creamy peanut butter**
- **2 teaspoons reduced-sodium soy sauce**
- **¼ teaspoon ground ginger**

1. Divide cabbage among four serving plates. Top with chicken, apple, and grapes. In a small bowl, whisk together the water, peanut butter, soy sauce, and ginger. Drizzle over salads. **Makes 4 (2¼-cup) servings.**

Chicken Salad
with Peanut Dressing

Mediterranean Tabbouleh Salad with Chicken

Mediterranean Tabbouleh Salad with Chicken

For a pick-up-and-eat salad, spoon the tabbouleh and chicken into the lettuce cups.

PER SERVING: 290 cal., 13 g total fat (2 g sat. fat), 72 mg chol., 275 mg sodium, 15 g carb., 4 g fiber, 30 g pro. Exchanges: 1.5 vegetable, 4 lean meat, 1.5 fat. Carb choices: 1

- **½ cup bulgur**
- **2 medium tomatoes, chopped**
- **1 cup finely chopped, seeded cucumber**
- **1 cup finely chopped fresh flat-leaf parsley**
- **⅓ cup thinly sliced green onions**
- **¼ cup snipped fresh mint or 1 tablespoon dried mint, crushed**
- **⅓ to ½ cup lemon juice**
- **¼ cup olive oil**
- **12 large leaves romaine and/or butterhead (Bibb or Boston) lettuce**
- **18 ounces grilled or broiled skinless, boneless chicken breast halves,* sliced**

1. In a large bowl, combine 1½ cups *water* and the bulgur. Let stand for 30 minutes. Drain bulgur through a fine sieve, using a large spoon to press out excess water. Return bulgur to bowl. Stir in tomatoes, cucumber, parsley, green onions, and mint.

2. For dressing, in a screw-top jar, combine lemon juice, oil, and ½ teaspoon each *salt* and *ground black pepper.* Cover and shake well. Pour dressing over the bulgur mixture. Toss lightly to coat. Cover and chill for 4 to 24 hours, stirring occasionally. Bring to room temperature before serving.

3. Serve romaine with bulgur mixture and cooked chicken. **Makes 6 servings (2 lettuce leaves, ⅔ cup bulgur mixture, and 3 ounces cooked chicken per serving).**

***To Grill Chicken:** Lightly sprinkle chicken with salt and ground black pepper. For a charcoal grill, place chicken on the grill rack directly over medium coals. Grill, uncovered, for 12 to 15 minutes or until chicken is no longer pink (170°F), turning once halfway through grilling. (For a gas grill, preheat grill. Reduce heat to medium. Place chicken on grill rack over heat. Cover and grill as above.)

***To Broil Chicken:** Preheat broiler. Lightly sprinkle chicken with salt and ground black pepper. Place chicken on the unheated rack of a broiler pan. Broil chicken 4 to 5 inches from heat for 12 to 15 minutes or until no longer pink (170°F), turning once halfway through broiling.

Salsa, Black Bean, and Rice Salad

This toss-together salad is perfect for a potluck.

PER SERVING: 153 cal., 1 g total fat (0 g sat. fat), 0 mg chol., 465 mg sodium, 32 g carb., 7 g fiber, 7 g pro. Exchanges: 1 vegetable, 1.5 starch. Carb choices: 2.

- **2 cups chopped romaine lettuce**
- **1½ cups cooked brown rice, chilled**
- **1 15-ounce can black beans, rinsed and drained**
- **2 cups chopped tomatoes**
- **1 cup chopped green, yellow, and/or red sweet pepper**
- **¾ cup frozen whole kernel corn, thawed**
- **2 green onions, thinly sliced**
- **2 tablespoons snipped fresh cilantro**
- **1 cup purchased picante sauce or salsa**
- **4 ounces Monterey Jack cheese with jalapeño chile peppers, cut into ¼-inch cubes (optional)**
- **6 small leaves romaine lettuce (optional)**
- **½ cup light dairy sour cream (optional)**

1. In a bowl, combine the 2 cups lettuce, the rice, beans, tomatoes, sweet pepper, corn, onions, and cilantro. Add picante sauce; toss to coat. If desired, stir in cheese. If desired, serve salad over lettuce leaves and serve with sour cream. **Makes 6 (1⅓-cup) servings.**

Salsa, Black Bean, and Rice Salad

(spill the beans)

The benefits of eating beans far outweigh the notorious side effects. Beans, including black, red, white, garbanzo, and navy, are naturally low in fat and contain no saturated fat, trans fat, or cholesterol. They are high in protein, fiber, iron, folic acid, and potassium. In addition to health benefits related to heart disease and cancer, studies suggest eating beans may help manage diabetes and cut the risk of high blood pressure and stroke. To reap the health benefits, serve beans as a main source of protein or as a side dish once or twice a week.

Apricot-Spinach Salad

Get a double shot of flavor with dried apricots in the salad and apricot nectar adding body to the ginger-soy dressing.

PER SERVING: 211 cal., 7 g total fat (1 g sat. fat), 0 mg chol., 336 mg sodium, 33 g carb., 8 g fiber, 9 g pro. Exchanges: 1 vegetable, 0.5 fruit, 1 starch, 0.5 lean meat, 1 fat. Carb choices: 2.

1 15-ounce can black beans, rinsed and drained
½ cup snipped dried apricots
1 cup red, orange, and/or yellow sweet pepper strips
2 tablespoons thinly sliced green onion
1 tablespoon snipped fresh cilantro
1 clove garlic, minced
¼ cup apricot nectar
2 tablespoons salad oil
2 tablespoons rice vinegar
1 teaspoon reduced-sodium soy sauce
1 teaspoon grated fresh ginger or ¼ teaspoon ground ginger
4 cups shredded fresh spinach
Green onion curls* or very thin strips green onion (optional)

1. In a medium bowl, combine black beans, apricots, sweet pepper, the 2 tablespoons green onion, the cilantro, and garlic. In a screw-top jar, combine apricot nectar, oil, rice vinegar, soy sauce, and ginger. Cover and shake well. Pour over bean mixture; toss gently to coat. Cover and chill for 2 to 24 hours.

2. To serve, arrange spinach in a salad bowl. Top with black bean mixture. If desired, garnish with additional green onion. **Makes 4 (1½-cup) servings.**

***Test Kitchen Tip:** To make green onion curls, soak thin strips of green onion in ice water for 30 to 60 minutes; drain and arrange on salad.

Southwest Salad

Double the ingredients to serve four.

PER SERVING: 165 cal., 4 g total fat (2 g sat. fat), 10 mg chol., 517 mg sodium, 23 g carb., 7 g fiber, 11 g pro. Exchanges: 2 vegetable, 1 starch, 0.5 medium-fat meat. Carb choices: 1.5.

- **2 cups torn mixed salad greens**
- **8 baked tortilla chips**
- **1 cup chopped yellow, red, and/or orange sweet pepper**
- **½ cup canned black beans, rinsed and drained**
- **½ cup chopped tomato**
- **¼ cup refrigerated fresh salsa**
- **¼ cup shredded reduced-fat cheddar cheese**
- **Freshly ground black pepper**

1. On two serving plates, layer salad greens and tortilla chips. In a bowl, combine sweet pepper, beans, tomato, and salsa. Spoon over chips. Top with cheese and sprinkle with black pepper. **Makes 2 (1½-cup) servings.**

Garden Greens with Tuna

Garden Greens with Tuna

To tote this simple salad for your lunch, pack the dressing in a separate container and drizzle it on just before eating.

PER SERVING: 206 cal., 5 g total fat (1 g sat. fat), 51 mg chol., 527 mg sodium, 10 g carb., 2 g fiber, 28 g pro. Exchanges: 2 fruit, 3 lean meat, 0.5 fat. Carb choices: 0.5.

- **1 pound fresh or frozen tuna steaks, cut 1 inch thick**
- **1 tablespoon lemon juice**
- **1 teaspoon dried Italian seasoning, crushed**
- **¼ teaspoon garlic salt**
- **⅛ teaspoon ground black pepper**
- **6 cups torn mixed salad greens**
- **2 medium red and/or yellow tomatoes, cut into wedges**
- **½ cup bottled light dried tomato vinaigrette salad dressing or light balsamic vinaigrette salad dressing**

1. Thaw fish, if frozen. Rinse fish; pat dry with paper towels. Brush fish with lemon juice. In a small bowl, stir together Italian seasoning, garlic salt, and pepper. Sprinkle mixture over fish.

2. Preheat broiler. Place fish on the greased unheated rack of a broiler pan. Broil 4 inches from heat for 8 to 12 minutes or until fish begins to flake when tested with a fork, gently turning once halfway through broiling. Cool; cut into chunks.

3. Divide salad greens among four serving plates. Top with fish and tomato wedges. Drizzle with vinaigrette. **Makes 4 servings.**

Salad Niçoise

Plunging the hot greens beans into ice water stops the cooking process and preserves the vibrant green color.

PER SERVING: 232 cal., 14 g total fat (3 g sat. fat), 124 mg chol., 595 mg sodium, 12 g carb., 5 g fiber, 16 g pro. Exchanges: 2.5 vegetable, 1.5 lean meat, 2 fat. Carb choices: 1.

- **4 ounces fresh green beans**
- **5 cups packaged European-style torn mixed salad greens**
- **1 6-ounce can chunk white tuna (water pack), drained and broken into chunks**
- **4 medium tomatoes, quartered**
- **2 hard-cooked eggs, quartered**
- **¾ cup pitted ripe olives**
- **½ cup snipped fresh flat-leaf parsley**

Salad Niçoise

- **3 green onions, cut into ½-inch-long pieces**
- **4 anchovy fillets, drained, rinsed, and patted dry (optional)**
- **1 recipe Niçoise Dressing (see recipe, below)**

1. Leave beans whole or snap in half. In a covered medium saucepan, cook green beans in a small amount of lightly salted boiling water about 5 minutes or just until tender. Drain and place in ice water until chilled; drain well. If desired, cover and chill for 2 to 24 hours.

2. In four salad bowls, arrange greens, green beans, tuna, tomatoes, eggs, and olives. Sprinkle with parsley and green onions. If desired, top with anchovy fillets. Drizzle Niçoise Dressing over salads. **Makes 4 servings.**

Niçoise Dressing: In a small bowl, combine 2 tablespoons olive oil, 2 tablespoons white wine vinegar, ½ teaspoon Dijon-style mustard, ¼ teaspoon salt, and ⅛ teaspoon ground black pepper. Whisk together until combined.

Seafood Salad with Ginger-Cream Dressing

A velvety dressing accented with ginger and orange brings out the best in tender scallops and succulent shrimp.

PER SERVING: 174 cal., 3 g total fat (1 g sat. fat), 86 mg chol., 184 mg sodium, 16 g carb., 2 g fiber, 22 g pro. Exchanges: 1 vegetable, 0.5 fruit, 3 lean meat. Carb choices: 1.

- **1 pound fresh or frozen sea scallops, cooked and chilled***
- **8 ounces fresh or frozen peeled and deveined shrimp, cooked and chilled ****
- **6 cups fresh spinach or torn mixed salad greens**
- **2 large mangoes or small papayas, seeded, peeled, and cut into chunks**
- **1 recipe Ginger-Cream Dressing (see recipe, right)**
- **2 tablespoons cashew halves or sliced almonds, toasted (optional)**

1. Halve any large scallops. In a large bowl, combine scallops, shrimp, spinach, and mangoes. Drizzle with Ginger-Cream Dressing; toss gently to coat.

2. To serve, divide the scallop mixture among six dinner plates. If desired, sprinkle with cashews. **Makes 6 servings.**

Ginger-Cream Dressing: In a small bowl, stir together 1/3 cup light dairy sour cream, 2 teaspoons grated fresh ginger or 1/2 teaspoon ground ginger, 1 teaspoon white wine vinegar, 1/2 teaspoon finely shredded orange peel, 1 teaspoon orange juice, and dash cayenne pepper.

Make-Ahead Directions: Prepare Ginger-Cream Dressing as directed. Cover and chill for up to 3 days.

*** Test Kitchen Tip:** To cook scallops, add 1/2 cup water to a large skillet. Bring to boiling. Add scallops. Return to boiling; reduce heat. Cover and simmer for 4 to 6 minutes or until scallops turn opaque. Drain and chill.

****Test Kitchen Tip:** If desired, leave the tails on shrimp. To cook shrimp, add 2 cups water to a medium saucepan. Bring to boiling. Add shrimp; return to boiling. Cook, uncovered, for 1 to 3 minutes or until shrimp turn opaque. Rinse under cold running water; drain and chill.

Seafood Salad with Ginger-Cream Dressing

Ginger Shrimp Pasta Salad

Let this Mediterranean feast stand at room temperature for 30 minutes before serving.

PER SERVING: 267 cal., 10 g total fat (1 g sat. fat), 97 mg chol., 122 mg sodium, 26 g carb., 2 g fiber, 17 g pro. Exchanges: 1 vegetable, 1.5 starch, 1.5very lean meat, 1.5 fat. Carb choices: 2.

- **1½ pounds fresh or frozen medium shrimp**
- **1 tablespoon olive oil**
- **2 cloves garlic, minced**
- **1 tablespoon grated fresh ginger**
- **8 ounces dried penne pasta**
- **¼ cup sherry vinegar or white wine vinegar**
- **¼ cup olive oil**
- **1½ cups halved yellow or red pear tomatoes or grape tomatoes**
- **1 cup chopped red or yellow sweet pepper**
- **1 stalk celery, finely chopped**
- **¼ cup finely chopped red onion**
- **¼ cup snipped fresh basil**
- **1 tablespoon capers, drained**
- **Ground black pepper**

1. Thaw shrimp, if frozen. Peel and devein shrimp, leaving tails intact. Rinse shrimp; pat dry with paper towels. In a large skillet, heat the 1 tablespoon oil over

Ginger Shrimp Pasta Salad

medium heat. Add garlic and ginger; cook and stir for 15 seconds. Add shrimp; cook about 3 minutes or until shrimp are opaque, stirring frequently. Set aside.

2. Meanwhile, cook pasta according to package directions. Drain. Rinse pasta with cold water; drain again.

3. In a very large bowl, whisk together vinegar and the 1/4 cup oil. Add cooked pasta and shrimp; toss to coat. Stir in tomatoes, sweet pepper, celery, red onion, basil, and capers. Season to taste with black pepper. Cover and chill for 2 to 24 hours. **Makes 8 (about 1-cup) servings.**

(clean greens)

Even though many salad greens can be purchased triple-washed, they should be washed again before using. To wash greens, first remove and discard roots, then separate the leaves. Swirl leaves around in a bowl filled with cold water about 30 seconds. Remove leaves and shake them gently to let dirt and other debris fall into the water. Repeat this process, using fresh water each time, until the water remains clear. Once washed, it's important to dry the greens. A salad spinner works wonders for this, but if you don't have one, pat each leaf dry with a clean paper towel.

Salmon Salad with Orange-Balsamic Vinaigrette

Salmon Salad with Orange-Balsamic Vinaigrette

Fresh salmon is often sold as a whole fillet. Ask the person at the fish counter to remove the skin and cut the salmon into the serving-size portions.

PER SERVING: 323 cal., 19 g total fat (3 g sat. fat), 66 mg chol., 296 mg sodium, 13 g carb., 3 g fiber, 24 g pro. Exchanges: 1 vegetable, 0.5 fruit, 3 lean meat, 3 fat. Carb choices: 1.

4 4- to 5-ounce fresh or frozen skinless salmon fillets
¼ teaspoon salt
¼ teaspoon ground black pepper
Nonstick cooking spray
2 tablespoons snipped fresh mint
2 tablespoons balsamic vinegar
2 tablespoons olive oil
¼ teaspoon finely shredded orange peel
2 tablespoons orange juice
⅛ teaspoon salt
5 cups packaged European-style torn mixed salad greens
2 oranges, thinly sliced
¼ of a medium red onion, thinly sliced
2 tablespoons sliced almonds, toasted (optional)

1. Thaw salmon, if frozen. Rinse salmon; pat dry with paper towels. Sprinkle salmon with the ¼ teaspoon salt and the pepper. Coat both sides of salmon fillets with nonstick cooking spray.

2. For a charcoal grill, place salmon on the grill rack directly over medium coals. Grill, uncovered, for 8 to 12 minutes or until salmon flakes easily when tested with a fork, turning once halfway through grilling. (For a gas grill, preheat grill. Reduce heat to medium. Place salmon on grill rack over heat. Cover and grill as above.)

3. Meanwhile, for vinaigrette, in a screw-top jar, combine mint, vinegar, oil, orange peel, orange juice, and the ⅛ teaspoon salt. Cover and shake well.

4. Divide salad greens among four serving plates. Top with orange slices and red onion. Top each salad with a salmon fillet. Drizzle with vinaigrette and, if desired, sprinkle with almonds. **Makes 4 servings.**

Quick Tip:

Try to incorporate at least two servings of fish that are high in omega-3 fatty acids, such as salmon, tuna, herring, mackerel, and lake trout, into your diet each week. Eating omega-3-rich salmon is believed to help fight heart disease, increase immunity, boost energy levels, and lift mood.

Creamy Creole Salmon on Greens

Start with salmon in a pouch, stir in a few ingredients, and have dinner on the table in minutes.

PER SERVING: 176 cal., 9 g total fat (3 g sat. fat), 41 mg chol., 710 mg sodium, 5 g carb., 1 g fiber, 19 g pro. Exchanges: 1 vegetable, 2.5 lean meat, 1 fat. Carb choices: 0.

2 7.1-ounce pouches skinless, boneless pink salmon, flaked
¼ cup chopped green onions
¼ cup light mayonnaise or salad dressing
1 tablespoon Creole mustard or spicy brown mustard
1 tablespoon ketchup
½ teaspoon bottled hot pepper sauce
5 cups torn mixed salad greens
Lemon wedges

1. In a medium bowl, stir together salmon, green onions, mayonnaise, mustard, ketchup, and hot pepper sauce.

2. Divide salad greens among four serving plates. Top greens with salmon mixture. Serve with lemon wedges. **Makes 4 (1¼ cups greens with about ½ cup salmon mixture per serving) servings.**

Sautéed Pork and Pear Salad

Pour any remaining pear nectar into ice cube trays and freeze for a later use.

PER SERVING: 246 cal., 10 g total fat (2 g sat. fat), 59 mg chol., 267 mg sodium, 19 g carb., 4 g fiber, 21 g pro. Exchanges: 1.5 vegetable, 2.5 lean meat, 2 fat. Carb choices: 1.

- **12 ounces boneless pork top loin roast or pork tenderloin, trimmed and cut into thin bite-size strips**
- **½ teaspoon dried sage, crushed**
- **Nonstick cooking spray**
- **¼ cup coarsely chopped almonds or hazelnuts (filberts)**
- **⅓ cup pear nectar**
- **1 tablespoon olive oil**
- **2 teaspoons Dijon-style mustard or chipotle chile pepper-style mustard**
- **6 cups torn mixed salad greens**
- **2 medium red and/or green pears, cored and sliced**

1. Sprinkle pork strips with sage and ¼ teaspoon each *salt* and *ground black pepper.* Coat an unheated large nonstick skillet with nonstick cooking spray. Preheat over medium-high heat. Add pork to hot skillet. Cook and stir for 2 to 3 minutes or until pork is slightly pink in the center. Add almonds. Cook and stir for 30 seconds more. Remove pork mixture. Cover and keep warm.

2. For dressing, carefully add nectar, oil, and mustard to hot skillet. Cook and stir just until blended, scraping up any crusty brown bits from bottom of skillet.

3. Divide salad greens and pear slices among four serving plates. Top with pork mixture; drizzle with warm dressing. Serve immediately. **Makes 4 servings.**

Sautéed Pork and Pear Salad

Lemon Sage Pork Taco Salad

Choose an avocado that yields to gentle pressure when cradled in your hand.

PER SERVING: 266 cal., 14 g total fat (2 g sat. fat), 49 mg chol., 269 mg sodium, 17 g carb., 7 g fiber, 21 g pro. Exchanges: 1.5 vegetable, 0.5 starch, 2.5 very lean meat, 2.5 fat. Carb choices: 1.

- **1 pound pork tenderloin**
- **1 tablespoon finely shredded lemon peel**
- **6 leaves fresh sage, thinly sliced**
- **½ teaspoon ground cumin**
- **1 tablespoon olive oil**
- **1 head green leaf lettuce, torn**
- **1½ cups chopped tomatoes**
- **1 avocado, halved, pitted, peeled, and chopped**
- **1 cup canned black beans, rinsed and drained**
- **½ cup chopped green onions**
- **Red Hot Pepper Vinaigrette (see recipe, below)**

1. Trim fat from pork. Cut pork crosswise into ¼-inch-thick slices. Place pork in a large bowl. Add lemon peel, sage, cumin, ¼ teaspoon *ground black pepper,* and ⅛ teaspoon *salt.* Toss well to coat. Let stand 10 minutes.

2. In a very large skillet, cook pork, half at a time, in hot oil over medium-high heat for 2 to 3 minutes or until meat is just slightly pink in center, turning once. Remove from skillet and set aside.

3. Place lettuce on a platter. Top with tomatoes, avocado, beans, and green onions. Arrange pork slices over salad. Drizzle with some Red Hot Pepper Vinaigrette; pass remaining vinaigrette. **Makes 6 (about 2-cup) servings.**

Red Hot Pepper Vinaigrette: Halve 1 red sweet pepper and 1 fresh jalapeño chile pepper (see tip, *page 30*) lengthwise. Remove stems, seeds, and membranes. Place pepper halves, cut sides down, on a foil-lined baking sheet. Bake in a 425°F oven for 20 to 25 minutes or until skin is blistered and charred. Bring foil up around peppers to enclose. Let stand 15 minutes. Use a sharp knife to pull off the skin in strips; discard. Place peppers in a blender or food processor. Add 2 tablespoons lime juice, 2 tablespoons balsamic vinegar, 2 tablespoons olive oil, and ⅛ teaspoon salt. Cover; blend until smooth.

Lemon Sage Pork Taco Salad

Middle Eastern Beef Salad

Spinach and Basil Salad with Beef

Middle Eastern Beef Salad

Give the measuring spoon a quick coating of nonstick cooking spray before pouring in the honey so all of the thick, sweet liquid will slide right out.

PER SERVING: 282 cal., 9 g total fat (3 g sat. fat), 58 mg chol., 542 mg sodium, 25 g carb., 6 g fiber, 27 g pro. Exchanges: 2 vegetable, 1 starch, 3 lean meat, 0.5 fat. Carb choices: 1.5.

12 ounces beef tenderloin steaks, cut 1 inch thick
⅛ teaspoon salt
⅛ teaspoon ground black pepper
6 cups packaged fresh baby spinach
2 medium yellow or red tomatoes, cut into wedges
1 small cucumber, coarsely chopped
1 15-ounce can garbanzo beans (chickpeas), rinsed and drained
¼ cup snipped fresh parsley
¼ cup snipped fresh mint
3 cloves garlic, minced
1 teaspoon olive oil
1 teaspoon honey
6 tablespoons plain low-fat or fat-free yogurt

1. Trim fat from steaks. Season steaks with salt and pepper. For a charcoal grill, place steaks on the grill rack directly over medium coals. Grill, uncovered, until desired doneness, turning once halfway through grilling. Allow 10 to 12 minutes for medium-rare doneness (145°F) or 12 to 15 minutes for medium (160°F). (For a gas grill, preheat grill. Reduce heat to medium. Place steaks on grill rack over heat. Cover and grill as above.)

2. Meanwhile, on a large serving platter, arrange spinach, tomatoes, cucumber, and garbanzo beans. Set aside.

3. For dressing, in a small bowl, combine parsley, mint, garlic, oil, and honey. Stir in yogurt until well combined.

4. Thinly slice the grilled steak and place on top of salad. Serve with dressing. **Makes 4 servings.**

Spinach and Basil Salad with Beef

Fresh oranges add a lively citrus zing.

PER SERVING: 311 cal., 15 g total fat (3 g sat. fat), 49 mg chol., 92 mg sodium, 14 g carb., 4 g fiber, 30 g pro. Exchanges: 1.5 vegetable, 0.5 fruit, 4 lean meat, 0.5 fat. Carb choices: 1.

¼ cup pear nectar
2 tablespoons canola oil
2 tablespoons white wine vinegar
½ teaspoon Worcestershire sauce for chicken
⅛ teaspoon freshly ground black pepper
4 cups packaged fresh baby spinach
2 cups sliced fresh mushrooms
½ cup lightly packed fresh basil leaves
12 ounces sliced cooked beef sirloin steak, cut into thin strips*
2 medium oranges, peeled and sectioned
¼ cup sliced almonds, toasted

1. For dressing, in a screw-top jar, combine pear nectar, oil, vinegar, Worcestershire sauce, and pepper. Cover and shake well.

2. In a bowl, toss together spinach, mushrooms, and basil leaves. Divide mixture among four serving plates. Top with beef strips; add orange sections. Drizzle with dressing and sprinkle with almonds. **Makes 4 servings.**

***Test Kitchen Tip:** To cook your own beef, start with 1 to 1¼ pounds boneless beef top sirloin steak, cut 1 inch thick. Preheat broiler. Place steak on the unheated rack of a broiler pan. Broil 3 to 4 inches from heat to desired doneness, turning once halfway through broiling. Allow 15 to 17 minutes for medium-rare doneness (145°F) or 20 to 22 minutes for medium doneness (160°F).

comforting soups and stews

Chipotle Chili with Hominy and Beans

A steaming bowl of hearty soup satisfies like nothing else. Whether you crave a brothy pasta soup, a tomatoey bean-filled chili, or a full-of-veggies stew, flip through these pages to discover soul-soothing, fill-you-up bowls of goodness.

Chipotle Chili with Hominy and Beans

Using no-salt-added tomatoes and rinsing the beans and hominy helps keep sodium levels in check.

PER SERVING: 257 cal., 7 g total fat (3 g sat. fat), 26 mg chol., 477 mg sodium, 35 g carb., 9 g fiber, 13 g pro. Exchanges: 1.5 vegetable, 1.5 starch, 1.5 very lean meat, 1 fat. Carb choices: 1.5.

Nonstick cooking spray
- **8 ounces 90% or higher lean ground beef or uncooked ground chicken or turkey breast**
- **1 cup chopped onion**
- **1½ teaspoons ground cumin**
- **½ teaspoon dried oregano, crushed**
- **2 14.5-ounce cans no-salt-added stewed tomatoes, undrained**
- **1 15-ounce can red beans, rinsed and drained**
- **1 15-ounce can yellow hominy, rinsed and drained**
- **1 small green or red sweet pepper, chopped**
- **½ cup water**
- **1 to 2 teaspoons chopped canned chipotle chile peppers in adobo sauce***
- **6 tablespoons shredded reduced-fat cheddar cheese (optional)**

1. Lightly coat an unheated large saucepan with nonstick cooking spray. Preheat over medium heat. Add ground beef and onion; cook until brown. If necessary, drain off fat.

2. Stir in cumin and oregano; cook for 1 minute more. Add undrained tomatoes, red beans, hominy, sweet pepper, the water, and chipotle peppers. Bring to boiling; reduce heat. Cover and simmer for 5 minutes. If desired, top each serving with cheddar cheese. **Makes 6 (1¼-cup) servings.**

***Test Kitchen Tip:** Because chile peppers contain volatile oils that can burn your skin and eyes, avoid direct contact with them as much as possible. When working with chile peppers, wear plastic or rubber gloves. If your bare hands do touch the peppers, wash your hands and nails well with soap and warm water.

Buffalo Vegetable Soup

If you use ground beef, omit the olive oil.

PER SERVING: 277 cal., 13 g total fat (5 g sat. fat), 53 mg chol., 443 mg sodium, 21 g carb., 3 g fiber, 19 g pro. Exchanges: 1 vegetable, 1 starch, 2 medium-fat meat. Carb choices: 1.5.

- **1 teaspoon olive oil**
- **1 pound ground bison (buffalo) or 90% or higher lean ground beef**
- **1 large onion, chopped**
- **1 fresh poblano pepper,* chopped**
- **4 cups reduced-sodium chicken broth**
- **2 medium potatoes, scrubbed and chopped**
- **1 cup frozen whole kernel corn**
- **1 medium red sweet pepper, seeded and chopped**
- **1 tablespoon snipped fresh sage or 1 teaspoon dried leaf sage, crushed**
- **2 teaspoons snipped fresh rosemary or ½ teaspoon dried rosemary, crushed**
- **2 medium zucchini, chopped**
- **Snipped fresh rosemary (optional)**

1. In a 4- to 5-quart Dutch oven, heat oil over medium heat. Add the ground bison, onion, and poblano pepper. Cook until meat is brown and onion is tender, stirring frequently to break up meat as it cooks. Drain off fat.

2. Add the broth, potatoes, corn, sweet pepper, and the dried sage and dried rosemary (if using). Bring just to boiling; reduce heat. Cover; simmer for 15 minutes.

3. Add zucchini, the fresh sage and fresh rosemary (if using), and ½ teaspoon *ground black pepper* to the soup; return to boiling. Reduce heat and simmer, covered, for 5 to 10 minutes or until vegetables are tender. If desired, sprinkle each serving with additional snipped fresh rosemary. **Makes 6 to 8 (1¼- to 1⅔-cup) servings.**

***Test Kitchen Tip:** Because chile peppers contain volatile oils that can burn your skin and eyes, avoid direct contact with them as much as possible. When working with chile peppers, wear plastic or rubber gloves. If your bare hands do touch the peppers, wash your hands and nails well with soap and warm water.

Three-Pepper Beef Stew

Cayenne pepper sauce, crushed red pepper, and red sweet peppers add up to triple-good flavor.

PER SERVING: 401 cal., 10 g total fat (3 g sat. fat), 82 mg chol., 358 mg sodium, 25 g carb., 4 g fiber, 36 g pro. Exchanges: 1.5 vegetable, 1 starch, 4.5 lean meat. Carb choices: 1.5.

- **1 tablespoon canola oil**
- **4 medium carrots, cut into 1-inch pieces**
- **2 stalks celery, cut into 1-inch pieces**
- **1 large onion, chopped**
- **6 cloves garlic, minced**
- **2 pounds beef chuck roast, trimmed of fat and cut into 1-inch cubes**
- **1¾ cups dry red wine or one 14-ounce can lower-sodium beef broth**
- **1 14-ounce can lower-sodium beef broth**
- **2 tablespoons tomato paste**
- **1 tablespoon Worcestershire sauce**
- **2 to 3 teaspoons bottled cayenne pepper sauce**
- **¼ to ½ teaspoon crushed red pepper**
- **2 large potatoes, unpeeled and cut into 1-inch pieces**
- **2 medium red sweet peppers, cut into 1-inch pieces**
- **1 tablespoon cornstarch**

1. In a 4- to 6-quart Dutch oven, heat oil over medium heat. Add carrots, celery, onion, and garlic; cook about 5 minutes or until onion is tender, stirring occasionally. Add beef; cook about 15 minutes or until brown, stirring occasionally. Drain off fat.

2. Stir in wine, broth, tomato paste, Worcestershire sauce, pepper sauce, and crushed red pepper. Bring to boiling; reduce heat. Cover and simmer 1 hour, stirring occasionally.

3. Add potatoes and sweet peppers. Return to boiling; reduce heat. Simmer, covered, for 15 to 20 minutes or until potatoes are tender. Stir together 2 tablespoons *cold water* and the cornstarch. Stir into beef mixture. Cook and stir until thickened and bubbly. Cook and stir for 2 minutes more. **Makes 6 (about 1½-cup) servings.**

Three-Pepper Beef Stew

Tex-Mex Pork and Corn Soup

Tex-Mex Pork and Corn Soup

For extra goodness, top each serving with a spoonful of light dairy sour cream and a sprinkle of snipped fresh cilantro.

PER SERVING: 192 cal., 5 g total fat (1 g sat. fat), 44 mg chol., 539 mg sodium, 21 g carb., 3 g fiber, 19 g pro. Exchanges: 0.5 vegetable, 1 starch, 2 lean meat, 0.5 fat. Carb choices: 1.5.

- **1 tablespoon olive oil**
- **12 ounces pork tenderloin or lean boneless pork, cut into bite-size pieces**
- **1 cup chopped red onion**
- **4 cloves garlic, minced**
- **1 10-ounce package frozen whole kernel corn**
- **1 14-ounce can reduced-sodium chicken broth**
- **1¾ cups water**
- **1 cup purchased chipotle-style salsa or regular salsa**
- **1 cup chopped red and/or yellow sweet pepper**
- **½ cup chopped tomato**

1. In a large saucepan, heat oil over medium-high heat. Add pork; cook and stir for 4 to 5 minutes or until brown and juices run clear. Remove pork from saucepan; set aside. Add red onion and garlic to saucepan. Cook and stir for 3 to 4 minutes or until onion is tender.

2. Add corn to saucepan. Cook and stir for 4 minutes. Stir in broth, the water, salsa, and sweet pepper. Bring to boiling; reduce heat. Simmer, uncovered, for 10 minutes. Return pork to saucepan; heat through. Remove saucepan from heat; stir in tomato. **Makes 5 (about 1⅓-cup) servings.**

Tex-Mex Chicken and Corn Soup: Prepare as above, except omit the pork and use 12 ounces skinless, boneless chicken breast halves, cut into 1-inch pieces.

PER SERVING: 192 cal., 5 g total fat (1 g sat. fat), 44 mg chol., 547 mg sodium, 21 g carb., 3 g fiber, 19 g pro. Exchanges: 0.5 vegetable, 1 starch, 2 lean meat, 0.5 fat. Carb choices 1.5.

Wild Rice-Ham Soup

Wild Rice-Ham Soup

Stack some spinach leaves and cut through to shred.

PER SERVING: 124 cal., 1 g total fat (0 g sat. fat), 11 mg chol., 584 mg sodium, 20 g carb., 3 g fiber, 10 g pro. Exchanges: 1 vegetable, 1 starch, 1 lean meat. Carb choices: 1.

- **5 cups water**
- **1 14-ounce can reduced-sodium chicken broth**
- **1 cup chopped celery**
- **5 ounces cooked ham, chopped (about 1 cup)**
- **¾ cup wild rice, rinsed and drained**
- **1 medium onion, cut into thin wedges**
- **1½ teaspoons dried thyme, crushed**
- **2 medium red sweet peppers, seeded and chopped**
- **4 cups shredded fresh spinach**

1. In a 4- to 5-quart slow cooker, combine the water, broth, celery, ham, uncooked wild rice, onion, and thyme.

2. Cover and cook on low-heat setting for 6 to 7 hours or on high-heat setting for 3 to 3½ hours.

3. If using low-heat setting, turn to high-heat setting. Stir in sweet peppers; cover and cook for 30 minutes more. Just before serving, stir in spinach. **Makes 6 (1½-cup) servings.**

Chicken-Tortellini Soup

Chicken-Tortellini Soup

Quick to make, this tasty soup is loaded with freshness.

PER SERVING: 265 cal., 6 g total fat (2 g sat. fat), 53 mg chol., 618 mg sodium, 30 g carb., 3 g fiber, 24 g pro. Exchanges: 1 vegetable, 2 starch, 2 very lean meat, 0.5 fat. Carb choices: 2.

2 teaspoons olive oil
12 ounces skinless, boneless chicken breast halves, cut into ¾-inch pieces
3 cloves garlic, minced
3 cups sliced fresh mushrooms (about 8 ounces)
2 14-ounce cans reduced-sodium chicken broth
1¾ cups water
1 9-ounce package refrigerated cheese-filled tortellini
2 medium carrots, cut into thin bite-size strips
2 cups torn fresh baby spinach
1 tablespoon snipped fresh tarragon

1. In a 4- to 6-quart Dutch oven, heat oil over medium-high heat. Add chicken and garlic; cook and stir about 4 minutes or until outsides of chicken pieces are no longer pink. Using a slotted spoon, remove chicken from Dutch oven.

2. Add mushrooms to the same Dutch oven. Cook about 5 minutes or just until tender, stirring frequently. Carefully add the broth and the water; bring to boiling. Add tortellini, carrots, and partially cooked chicken to broth mixture. Return to boiling; reduce heat. Cover and simmer for 7 to 9 minutes or until tortellini is tender, stirring occasionally. Stir in spinach and tarragon. **Makes 6 (1⅓-cup) servings.**

Chicken Minestrone Soup

Grab a Microplane and a chunk of Parmesan cheese and shred a little over each bowl for an Italian accent.

PER SERVING: 167 cal., 3 g total fat (0 g sat. fat), 16 mg chol., 583 mg sodium, 27 g carb., 7 g fiber, 15 g pro. Exchanges: 1 vegetable, 1.5 starch, 1 lean meat. Carb choices: 2.

1 tablespoon olive oil
1 cup sliced carrots
½ cup chopped celery
½ cup chopped onion
2 14-ounce cans reduced-sodium chicken broth
2 15-ounce cans cannellini beans (white kidney beans), rinsed and drained
1¾ cups water
8 ounces skinless, boneless chicken breast halves, cut into bite-size pieces
1 cup fresh green beans, cut into ½-inch pieces (4 ounces)
¼ teaspoon ground black pepper
1 cup dried bow tie pasta
1 medium zucchini, quartered lengthwise and cut into ½-inch-thick slices
1 14.5-ounce can diced tomatoes with basil, garlic, and oregano, undrained

1. In a 5- to 6-quart Dutch oven, heat oil over medium heat. Add carrots, celery, and onion; cook for 5 minutes, stirring frequently. Add broth, cannellini beans, water, chicken, green beans, and pepper. Bring to boiling; add uncooked pasta. Reduce heat; simmer, uncovered, for 5 minutes.

2. Stir in zucchini. Return to boiling; reduce heat. Simmer, uncovered, for 8 to 10 minutes more or until pasta is tender and green beans are crisp-tender. Stir in undrained tomatoes; heat through. **Makes 8 (about 1⅓-cup) servings.**

(keep it hot)

Soup tastes best when served hot. To keep it from cooling down too quickly, serve it in warmed bowls. To warm the bowls, preheat your oven to 200°F, turn it off, and place the bowls in a single layer on the oven rack for a few minutes to warm. Or pour boiling water into the bowls and let them stand for a few minutes. Discard the water and dry the bowls before adding the soup.

Chicken Minestrone Soup

Caraway Chicken and Vegetable Stew

Caraway Chicken and Vegetable Stew

The stems of shiitake and oyster mushrooms are woody and tough. Be sure to remove and discard them before slicing the caps.

PER SERVING: 163 cal., 5 g total fat (1 g sat. fat), 63 mg chol., 410 mg sodium, 12 g carb., 3 g fiber, 19 g pro. Exchanges: 1.5 vegetable, 1 fat, 2 lean meat. Carb choices: 1.

- **2 teaspoons olive oil**
- **1 pound skinless, boneless chicken thighs or breast halves, trimmed of fat and cut into 1½-inch pieces**
- **2 14-ounce cans reduced-sodium chicken broth**
- **8 ounces fresh green beans, trimmed and cut into 2-inch-long pieces**
- **2 medium carrots, bias-cut into ½-inch-thick slices**
- **2 stalks celery, bias-cut into ½-inch-thick slices**
- **2 cups sliced fresh shiitake, cremini, oyster, and/or button mushrooms**
- **1 cup frozen pearl onions**
- **1¼ teaspoons caraway seeds, crushed**
- **¼ teaspoon ground black pepper**
- **¼ cup cold water**
- **2 tablespoons cornstarch**

1. In a 4-quart Dutch oven, heat oil over medium-high heat. Add chicken; cook for 3 to 5 minutes or until brown, stirring occasionally. Add broth, green beans, carrots, celery, mushrooms, onions, caraway seeds, and pepper. Bring to boiling; reduce heat. Cover and simmer for 10 minutes or until vegetables are tender and chicken is no longer pink.

2. In a small bowl, combine the water and the cornstarch; whisk until smooth. Add to stew. Cook and stir until thickened and bubbly. Cook and stir for 2 minutes more. **Makes 6 (1¼-cup) servings.**

Yucatan-Style Turkey and Vegetable Soup

Queso fresco is a mild Mexican cheese with a crumbly texture similar to that of feta or farmer's cheese. Look for it at Hispanic food markets or larger supermarkets.

PER SERVING: 229 cal., 8 g total fat (2 g sat. fat), 65 mg chol., 609 mg sodium, 12 g carb., 4 g fiber, 27 g pro. Exchanges: 1.5 vegetable, 3.5 very lean meat, 1.5 fat. Carb choices: 1.

- **1 medium onion, thinly sliced**
- **3 or 4 unpeeled cloves garlic**
- **1 tablespoon cooking oil**
- **2 canned chipotle chile peppers in adobo sauce, drained and chopped (see tip, page 61)**
- **2 medium carrots, chopped**
- **5 cups reduced-sodium chicken broth or turkey stock**
- **2 cups coarsely chopped tomatoes**
- **1 pound cooked turkey, cubed or shredded (3 cups)**
- **2 small zucchini, chopped (2 cups)**
- **2 tablespoons snipped fresh cilantro**
- **⅓ cup crumbled queso fresco or feta cheese**
- **1 avocado, halved, pitted, peeled, and chopped**
- **Thin strips fresh lime peel (optional)**
- **1 lime, cut into wedges (optional)**

1. In a dry medium skillet, combine onion and garlic cloves; cook and stir for 3 to 5 minutes or until edges are brown. Chop onion; peel and slice garlic cloves.

2. In a 4-quart Dutch oven, heat oil over medium-high heat. Add chopped onion, sliced garlic, and chipotle peppers; cook and stir for 3 minutes. Add carrots; cook and stir for 3 minutes more. Add broth, tomatoes, and ⅛ teaspoon *salt*. Bring to boiling; reduce heat. Cover and simmer for 10 minutes. Add turkey, zucchini, and cilantro; cover and cook for 5 minutes more.

3. Top each serving with queso fresco, avocado, and, if desired, lime peel strips. If desired, serve with lime wedges. **Makes 6 (1⅔-cup) servings.**

Yucatan-Style Turkey and Vegetable Soup

Pizza Soup

Pizza Soup

Crowned with cheese, this bowl resembles a piece of America's favorite pie—pizza!

PER SERVING: 174 cal., 8 g total fat (2 g sat. fat), 24 mg chol., 388 mg sodium, 19 g carb., 4 g fiber, 10 g pro. Exchanges: 2 vegetable, 0.5 carb., 1 medium-fat meat, 0.5 fat. Carb choices: 1.

- **1 tablespoon olive oil**
- **1 cup chopped onion**
- **1 cup chopped green sweet pepper**
- **1 cup sliced fresh mushrooms**
- **3 cloves garlic, minced**
- **1 14.5-ounce can no-salt-added diced tomatoes, undrained**
- **1 8-ounce can no-salt-added tomato sauce**
- **1¾ cups water**
- **1 small zucchini, halved lengthwise and sliced**
- **4 ounces smoked turkey sausage, halved lengthwise and thinly sliced**
- **2 teaspoons dried Italian seasoning, crushed**
- **½ teaspoon pizza seasoning**
- **¼ cup shredded part-skim mozzarella cheese (1 ounce)**

1. In a large saucepan, heat oil over medium heat. Add onion, sweet pepper, mushrooms, and garlic; cook about 5 minutes or until vegetables are lightly golden brown, stirring occasionally. Stir in undrained tomatoes, tomato sauce, the water, zucchini, sausage, Italian seasoning, and pizza seasoning. Return to boiling; reduce heat. Simmer, uncovered, for 5 to 10 minutes or until vegetables are tender. Top each serving with cheese. **Makes 4 (1½-cup) servings.**

Turkey and Sweet Potato Chowder

This recipe is a terrific way to use leftover holiday turkey. If you don't have any, buy a cooked turkey breast half or substitute chopped cooked chicken.

PER SERVING: 229 cal., 1 g total fat (0 g sat. fat), 58 mg chol., 279 mg sodium, 29 g carb., 2 g fiber, 27 g pro. Exchanges: 2 starch, 2.5 very lean meat. Carb choices: 2.

- **1 large potato, peeled, if desired, and chopped (about 1½ cups)**
- **1 14-ounce can reduced-sodium chicken broth**
- **2 small ears frozen corn on the cob, thawed, or 1 cup frozen whole kernel corn**
- **1 medium sweet potato, peeled and cut into ¾-inch cubes (about 1½ cups)**
- **1 teaspoon snipped fresh thyme or ¼ teaspoon dried thyme, crushed**
- **⅛ to ¼ teaspoon ground black pepper**
- **12 ounces cooked turkey breast, cut into ½-inch cubes (about 2¼ cups)**
- **1½ cups fat-free milk**

1. In a 3-quart saucepan, combine chopped potato and broth. Bring to boiling; reduce heat. Simmer, uncovered, about 12 minutes or until potato is tender, stirring occasionally. Remove from heat. Do not drain. Using a potato masher, mash potato until mixture is thickened and nearly smooth.

2. If using corn on the cob, carefully cut crosswise into ½-inch-thick slices.

3. Stir corn pieces or frozen corn kernels, sweet potato, dried thyme (if using), and pepper into potato mixture in saucepan. Bring to boiling; reduce heat. Cover and simmer for 12 to 15 minutes or until the sweet potato is tender. Stir in turkey and milk; heat through.

4. To serve, ladle chowder into bowls. Sprinkle with fresh thyme (if using). **Makes 5 (1⅓-cup) servings.**

Quick Tip:

If you know you are going to have a busy week, do your grocery shopping in advance and prep some of the foods for the week. Veggies can be chopped and cheeses can be shredded ahead and stored in resealable bags or airtight containers in the refrigerator.

Turkey and Sweet Potato Chowder

Pepper-Corn Chowder

Saffron gives this garden-fresh chowder a deliciously sophisticated flavor. Vegetables add healthful fiber.

PER SERVING: 126 cal., 1 g total fat (0 g sat. fat), 0 mg chol., 245 mg sodium, 29 g carb., 4 g fiber, 5 g pro. Exchanges: 0.5 vegetable, 1.5 starch. Carb choices: 2.

- **10 ears fresh corn or 5 cups frozen whole kernel corn**
- **Nonstick cooking spray**
- **1 cup chopped onion**
- **1 leek, cleaned and chopped**
- **2 14-ounce cans reduced-sodium chicken broth**
- **1 medium red sweet pepper, chopped**
- **⅛ teaspoon ground black pepper**
- **⅛ teaspoon cayenne pepper**
- **3 threads saffron (optional)**

1. If using fresh corn, with a sharp knife, cut kernels off cobs by cutting along the cob across the base of the kernels from the top end to the bottom end. You should have about 5 cups corn kernels. Set aside.

2. Coat a 4- to 5-quart Dutch oven with nonstick cooking spray. Preheat over medium heat about 1 minute. Add onion and leek; cook about 5 minutes or until tender, stirring occasionally.

3. Add corn. Cook about 5 minutes or until corn softens, stirring occasionally. Add 1 can of the chicken broth. Heat to boiling; reduce heat. Cover and simmer about 25 minutes or until the corn is very tender. Remove from heat and cool slightly.

4. Transfer half the corn mixture to a blender or food processor; cover and blend until smooth. Return the pureed corn mixture to the mixture in Dutch oven.

5. Add the remaining 1 can broth, the sweet pepper, black pepper, cayenne pepper, and, if desired, saffron. Heat through. **Makes 8 (about 1-cup) servings.**

Red Bean Stew

A quartet of flavors—garlic, cilantro, oregano, and adobo seasoning—adds a zesty kick to this satisfying vegetarian meal in a bowl.

PER SERVING: 220 cal., 2 g total fat (0 g sat. fat), 0 mg chol., 427 mg sodium, 44 g carb., 8 g fiber, 11 g pro. Exchanges: 2.5 starch, 0.5 very lean meat. Carb choices: 3.

- **1 teaspoon cooking oil**
- **⅔ cup chopped red onion**

Red Bean Stew

- **3 cloves garlic, minced**
- **1 cup water**
- **2 tablespoons tomato paste**
- **1 tablespoon snipped fresh cilantro**
- **1 teaspoon snipped fresh oregano or ¼ teaspoon dried oregano, crushed**
- **½ teaspoon adobo seasoning***
- **1 15-ounce can red kidney beans, rinsed and drained**
- **2 cups hot cooked brown rice**
- **Fresh cilantro sprigs (optional)**

1. In a large skillet, heat oil over medium heat. Add red onion and garlic; cook about 5 minutes or until onion is tender. Carefully add the water, tomato paste, the snipped cilantro, the oregano, and adobo seasoning. Stir in beans. Bring to boiling; reduce heat. Cook and stir over medium heat for 5 to 10 minutes or until soup is slightly thickened, mashing beans slightly while stirring.

2. Serve stew with rice. If desired, garnish with cilantro sprigs. **Makes 4 servings (½ cup stew and ½ cup rice per serving).**

***Test Kitchen Tip:** Look for this seasoning blend at a market that specializes in Hispanic foods.

(lovely leeks)

Leeks look like large green onions but have a more distinctive flavor. Look for those with leaves that are crisp and healthy looking. Leek bulbs that are 1½ inches or smaller in diameter are more tender than the larger leeks. Leeks often have dirt within the layers, so be sure to clean them thoroughly. Use a chef's knife to cut a thin slice from the root end of the leek. Cut off the dark green leaves and remove any wilted outer leaves. Then cut the leek lengthwise in half. To wash, hold the leek halves under cool running water, separating and lifting the leaves with your fingers to make sure that all of the dirt is rinsed away.

Green Garden Minestrone

Because of all the veggie options, you can make this hearty but simple soup with your favorites.

PER SERVING: 85 cal., 2 g total fat (0 g sat. fat), 0 mg chol., 321 mg sodium, 13 g carb., 3 g fiber, 5 g pro. Exchanges: 1.5 vegetable, 0.5 starch. Carb choices: 1.

1 tablespoon olive oil
1 cup sliced celery
⅔ cup finely chopped leeks
6 green onions, sliced
1 clove garlic, finely chopped
4 cups reduced-sodium chicken broth or stock
2 cups water
1½ cups sliced fresh green beans and/or fresh or frozen green peas
½ cup dried tiny shell pasta
¼ teaspoon ground black pepper
1 pound asparagus spears, trimmed and thinly sliced, and/or 8 ounces baby zucchini, sliced
6 cups fresh baby spinach leaves, coarsely chopped, or 1½ cups finely shredded green cabbage
¼ cup snipped fresh basil
½ cup thinly shaved Parmesan cheese (optional)

1. In a 4-quart Dutch oven, heat oil over medium heat. Add celery, leeks, green onions, and garlic; cook until crisp-tender, stirring occasionally.

2. Add broth, the water, green beans and/or peas, pasta, and pepper. Heat to boiling; reduce heat. Simmer, uncovered, for 10 minutes. Stir in the asparagus and/or zucchini and spinach; simmer for 2 to 3 minutes more or until pasta and vegetables are tender. Stir in basil.

3. If desired, top each serving with Parmesan cheese. **Makes 8 (1-cup) servings.**

Green Garden Minestrone

Zesty Gazpacho

Thai Shrimp Soup

Zesty Gazpacho

Be sure the bowl you use for mixing this gazpacho is made of a nonreactive material, such as glass.

PER SERVING: 152 cal., 1 g total fat (0 g sat. fat), 0 mg chol., 605 mg sodium, 37 g carb., 10 g fiber, 10 g pro. Exchanges: 3.5 vegetable, 1 starch. Carb choices: 2.5.

- **1 19-ounce can cannellini beans (white kidney beans), rinsed and drained**
- **1 14.5-ounce can Italian- or Mexican-style stewed tomatoes, undrained and cut up**
- **2 cups tiny red pear-shape or cherry tomatoes, halved or quartered**
- **1 11.5-ounce can low-sodium vegetable juice**
- **1 cup water**
- **1 cup coarsely chopped seeded cucumber**
- **½ cup coarsely chopped seeded yellow and/or red sweet pepper**
- **¼ cup coarsely chopped red onion**
- **¼ cup snipped fresh cilantro**
- **3 tablespoons lime juice or lemon juice**
- **2 cloves garlic, minced**
- **¼ to ½ teaspoon bottled hot pepper sauce**

1. In a large bowl, combine cannellini beans, undrained stewed tomatoes, fresh tomatoes, vegetable juice, the water, cucumber, sweet pepper, red onion, cilantro, lime juice, garlic, and hot pepper sauce. Cover and chill for 2 to 24 hours. **Makes 4 (2-cup) servings.**

Thai Shrimp Soup

If you wish, use brown sugar substitute equivalent to 2 teaspoons brown sugar in this recipe.

PER SERVING: 146 cal., 2 g total fat (0 g sat. fat), 129 mg chol., 623 mg sodium, 11 g carb., 2 g fiber, 20 g pro. Exchanges: 1 vegetable, 0.5 carb., 2.5 lean meat. Carb choices: 1.

- **12 ounces fresh or frozen peeled and deveined shrimp (tails intact if desired)**
- **1 14-ounce can reduced-sodium chicken broth**
- **2 stalks lemongrass (white part only), cut into ½-inch-thick slices**
- **2 medium fresh jalapeño chile peppers, halved lengthwise and seeded***
- **1 cup stemmed and sliced fresh shiitake and/or button mushrooms or ½ of a 15-ounce can whole straw mushrooms, drained**
- **1 cup chopped red sweet pepper**
- **1 cup sliced carrots**
- **2 tablespoons lime juice**
- **2 tablespoons rice vinegar or white wine vinegar**
- **2 teaspoons packed brown sugar**
- **2 teaspoons bottled fish sauce**
- **¼ cup slivered fresh basil**

1. Thaw shrimp, if frozen. Rinse shrimp; pat dry with paper towels. Set aside. In a large saucepan, combine broth and 2¾ cups *water;* bring to boiling. Add lemongrass and chile peppers. Return to boiling; reduce heat. Cover; simmer for 10 minutes. Use a slotted spoon to remove lemongrass and chile peppers; discard.

2. Stir mushrooms, sweet pepper, carrots, lime juice, rice vinegar, brown sugar, and fish sauce into liquid in saucepan. Bring to boiling; reduce heat. Cover and simmer for 10 to 15 minutes or until vegetables are crisp-tender. Add shrimp. Cook, covered, for 2 to 4 minutes more or until shrimp are opaque. Sprinkle each serving with basil. **Makes 4 (1½-cup) servings.**

***Test Kitchen Tip:** Because chile peppers contain volatile oils that can burn your skin and eyes, avoid direct contact with them as much as possible. When working with chile peppers, wear plastic or rubber gloves. If your bare hands do touch the peppers, wash your hands and nails well with soap and warm water.

Thai Tofu Soup: Prepare as above, except omit shrimp and use 12 ounces firm, silken-style tofu (fresh bean curd), cut into bite-size pieces.

PER SERVING: 106 cal., 3 g total fat (0 g sat. fat), 0 mg chol., 527 mg sodium, 13 g carb., 2 g fiber, 9 g pro. Exchanges: 1 vegetable, 0.5 carb., 1 medium-fat meat. Carb choices: 1.

sensational sandwiches

Tomato-Basil Panini

If your day seems too busy to get a meal on the table, choose sandwiches—they're the go-to entrée when you're in a hurry. Easy to make and even easier to eat, sandwiches of all sorts are great on-the-go meals. Best of all, everybody loves 'em.

Tomato-Basil Panini

There are several choices of cookware to use to create this gooey, delicious toasted sandwich.

PER PANINI: 174 cal., 5 g total fat (2 g sat. fat), 5 mg chol., 597 mg sodium, 27 g carb., 5 g fiber, 10 g pro. Exchanges: 1 vegetable, 1.5 starch, 0.5 lean meat. Carb choices: 2.

Olive oil nonstick cooking spray
8 slices whole wheat bread; four 6-inch whole wheat hoagie rolls, split; or 2 whole wheat pita bread rounds, halved crosswise and split horizontally
4 cups packaged fresh baby spinach
1 medium tomato, cut into 8 slices
⅛ teaspoon salt
⅛ teaspoon ground black pepper
¼ cup thinly sliced red onion
2 tablespoons shredded fresh basil
½ cup crumbled reduced-fat feta cheese (2 ounces)

1. Lightly coat an unheated electric sandwich press, panini griddle, covered indoor grill, grill pan, or large nonstick skillet with nonstick cooking spray; set aside.

2. Place 4 of the bread slices, roll bottoms, or pita pieces on a work surface; divide half of the spinach among these bread slices, roll bottoms, or pita pieces. Top spinach with tomato; sprinkle lightly with salt and pepper. Add red onion and basil. Top with feta and the remaining spinach. Top with the remaining bread slices, roll tops, or pita pieces. Press down firmly.

3. Preheat sandwich press, panini griddle, or covered indoor grill according to manufacturer's directions. (Or heat grill pan or skillet over medium heat.) Add sandwiches, in batches if necessary. If using sandwich press, panini griddle, or covered indoor grill, close lid and grill for 2 to 3 minutes or until bread is toasted. (If using grill pan or skillet, place a heavy skillet on top of sandwiches. Cook over medium heat for 1 to 2 minutes or until bottoms are toasted. Carefully remove top skillet, which may be hot. Turn sandwiches and top again with the skillet. Cook for 1 to 2 minutes more or until bread is toasted.) **Makes 4 panini.**

Quick Tip:

When a yummy filling, like this creamy egg and veggie salad, along with fresh lettuce and tomatoes get rolled into a wrap, the tortilla sometimes likes to unroll, making it a mess to eat. Use a toothpick or sandwich pick to help secure the tortilla around the filling.

Egg and Vegetable Salad Wraps

Egg and Vegetable Salad Wraps

Veggies turn the often high-fat egg salad into one that's more healthful—brimming with vitamins and antioxidants.

PER WRAP: 235 cal., 10 g total fat (3 g sat. fat), 162 mg chol., 517 mg sodium, 21 g carb., 11 g fiber, 14 g pro. Exchanges: 1 vegetable, 1 starch, 1 medium-fat meat, 1 fat. Carb choices: 1.5.

3 hard-cooked eggs, peeled and chopped
½ cup chopped cucumber
½ cup chopped zucchini or yellow summer squash
¼ cup chopped red onion
¼ cup shredded carrot
2 tablespoons light mayonnaise or salad dressing
1 tablespoon Dijon-style mustard
2 teaspoons fat-free milk
½ teaspoon snipped fresh basil or ¼ teaspoon dried basil, crushed
Dash paprika
4 leaf lettuce leaves
4 7- to 8-inch whole grain, spinach, or vegetable flour tortillas
1 roma tomato, thinly sliced

1. In a large bowl, combine eggs, cucumber, zucchini, red onion, and carrot. For dressing, in a small bowl, stir together mayonnaise, mustard, milk, basil, and paprika. Pour dressing over egg mixture; toss gently to coat.

2. For each wrap, place a lettuce leaf on a tortilla. Top with tomato slices, slightly off center. Spoon egg mixture on tomato slices. Fold bottom edge of each tortilla up and over the filling. Roll tortillas around filling. **Makes 4 wraps.**

Grilled Vegetable Pitas

Perfect for outdoor dining, these pitas pockets filled with grilled vegetables and tangy feta cheese make for easy no-utensil noshing.

PER SERVING: 188 cal., 6 g total fat (2 g sat. fat), 7 mg chol., 560 mg sodium, 26 g carb., 4 g fiber, 10 g pro. Exchanges: 1 vegetable, 1.5 starch, 0.5 medium-fat meat. Carb choices: 2.

1 4-ounce fresh portobello mushroom
1 tablespoon balsamic vinegar
1 teaspoon olive oil
Dash salt and ground black pepper
¼ of a medium yellow or red sweet pepper, stem and seeds removed

Grilled Vegetable Pitas

¼ cup chopped tomato
1 large whole wheat pita bread round, halved crosswise
8 fresh spinach leaves
8 small fresh basil leaves
⅓ cup crumbled reduced-fat feta cheese

1. If present, remove and discard mushroom stem. If desired, remove mushroom gills. In a small bowl, combine balsamic vinegar, oil, salt, and black pepper. Gently brush half of the oil mixture over mushroom and sweet pepper.

2. For a charcoal grill, place mushroom and sweet pepper on the grill rack directly over medium coals. Grill, uncovered, for 10 to 12 minutes or until the vegetables are lightly charred and tender, turning frequently. (For a gas grill, preheat grill. Reduce heat to medium. Place mushroom and sweet pepper on grill rack over heat. Cover and grill as above.)

3. Meanwhile, in a medium bowl, combine the remaining oil mixture and the tomato; toss gently to coat. Cut grilled mushroom and sweet pepper into bite-size strips. Add mushroom and pepper strips to tomato mixture; toss gently to combine.

4. Open pita halves to create pockets. Line pita pockets with spinach and basil. Fill pita pockets with grilled vegetable mixture. Sprinkle with cheese. Serve immediately. **Makes 2 servings.**

Seasoned Tuna Sandwiches

Seasoned Tuna Sandwiches

Look for capers next to the olives in the supermarket. Try stirring a few in red pasta sauce, sprinkling some over grilled fish, or tossing them in a salad.

PER SANDWICH: 277 cal., 8 g total fat (1 g sat. fat), 48 mg chol., 446 mg sodium, 23 g carb., 4 g fiber, 28 g pro. Exchanges: 0.5 vegetable, 1.5 starch, 3 lean meat, 0.5 fat. Carb choices: 1.5.

- **2 6-ounce cans low-sodium chunk (light or white) tuna, drained**
- **2 teaspoons lemon juice**
- **1 tablespoon olive oil**
- **1 teaspoon capers, drained**
- **⅛ teaspoon ground black pepper**
- **2 tablespoons light mayonnaise or salad dressing**
- **8 slices whole wheat bread, toasted**
- **4 romaine lettuce leaves, ribs removed**
- **4 large tomato slices**

1. In a small bowl, combine tuna, lemon juice, oil, capers, and pepper.

2. To assemble sandwiches, spread mayonnaise on 4 of the bread slices. Top with lettuce, tomato, tuna mixture, and remaining bread slices. **Makes 4 sandwiches.**

Tuna-Red Pepper Salad Wraps

Forget the tortilla here. Leaves of butterhead lettuce serve as the wrappers for this light tuna salad.

PER SERVING: 216 cal., 11 g total fat (2 g sat. fat), 48 mg chol., 599 mg sodium, 10 g carb., 2 g fiber, 19 g pro. Exchanges: 1 vegetable, 0.5 starch, 2.5 lean meat, 1 fat. Carb choices: 0.5.

- **1 5-ounce pouch chunk light tuna**
- **¼ cup light mayonnaise**
- **¼ cup chopped bottled roasted red sweet peppers**
- **1 tablespoon chopped sweet gherkins**
- **6 butterhead (Boston or Bibb) lettuce leaves**
- **1 slice whole wheat bread, toasted and cut into 6 strips**

1. In a small bowl, combine tuna, mayonnaise, red peppers, and gherkins. Spoon tuna mixture onto each lettuce leaf near one edge. Top each with a strip of toast. Roll up lettuce, starting from the edge with the tuna mixture. **Makes 2 servings (3 lettuce wraps each).**

Veggie Burger Fix-Ups

Meatless burgers from the freezer case go gourmet with your choice of these three stir-together toppers.

PER BURGER WITH 1 TABLESPOON ULTRA KETCHUP TOPPER: 200 cal., 2 g total fat (0 g sat. fat), 0 mg chol., 607 mg sodium, 31 g carb., 6 g fiber, 17 g pro. Exchanges: 2 starch, 1.5 lean meat. Carb choices: 2.

- **6 refrigerated or frozen plain or flavored meatless burger patties**
- **6 whole wheat hamburger buns, toasted**
- **1 recipe Ultra Ketchup Topper, Smoky Berry Topper, or Double Pepper Topper**

1. Heat burgers according to package directions. Place heated burgers on bun bottoms. Top burgers with desired topper. Top with bun tops. **Makes 6 burgers.**

Ultra Ketchup Topper: In a bowl, combine ¼ cup ketchup; 4 teaspoons chopped, drained oil-pack dried tomatoes; 1 teaspoon red wine vinegar; 1 teaspoon packed brown sugar; and dash ground black pepper. Try with roasted onion-flavor burger and top with sliced tomatoes.

Smoky Berry Topper: In a small bowl, mash ¾ cup blueberries and/or raspberries with a potato masher or fork. Add 2 tablespoons cider vinegar and 2 slices crisp-cooked and crumbled bacon (stir in bacon just before serving). Try with roasted garlic-flavor burger and top with fresh watercress.

PER BURGER WITH 2 TABLESPOONS SMOKY BERRY TOPPER: 204 cal., 3 g total fat (0 g sat. fat), 5 mg chol., 603 mg sodium, 30 g carb., 6 g fiber, 18 g pro. Exchanges: 2 starch, 1.5 very lean meat. Carb choices: 2.

Double Pepper Topper: In a small bowl, combine ¾ cup chopped, drained bottled roasted red sweet peppers; 1 tablespoon adobo sauce from canned chipotle peppers in adobo sauce; 1 tablespoon sherry vinegar; and 1 teaspoon sugar. Try with grilled vegetable-flavor burger and top with shredded yellow summer squash.

PER BURGER WITH 2 TABLESPOONS DOUBLE PEPPER TOPPER: 194 cal., 2 g total fat (0 g sat. fat), 0 mg chol., 503 mg sodium, 30 g carb., 7 g fiber, 17 g pro. Exchanges: 2 starch, 1.5 very lean meat. Carb choices: 2.

Veggie Burger Fix-Ups

Cannellini Bean Burgers

Cannellini Bean Burgers

To make the soft bread crumbs, tear a slice of fresh bread into pieces and give it a whirl in a food processor.

PER BURGER: 280 cal., 12 g total fat (1 g sat. fat), 2 mg chol., 394 mg sodium, 37 g carb., 11 g fiber, 14 g pro. Exchanges: 1 vegetable, 2 starch, 1 lean meat, 1 fat. Carb choices: 2.5.

- **1 15- to 16-ounce can cannellini (white kidney) beans, rinsed and drained**
- **¾ cup soft whole wheat bread crumbs (1 slice)**
- **½ cup chopped onion**
- **¼ cup walnut pieces, toasted if desired**
- **2 tablespoons coarsely chopped fresh basil or 1 teaspoon dried basil, crushed**
- **2 cloves garlic, quartered**
- **1 tablespoon olive oil**
- **4 slices whole grain bread, toasted**
- **2 tablespoons bottled light ranch salad dressing**
- **2 cups fresh spinach**
- **4 tomato slices, halved**

1. In a food processor, combine beans, ¼ cup of the bread crumbs, the onion, nuts, basil, and garlic. Process until mixture is coarsely chopped and holds together.

2. Shape bean mixture into four ½-inch-thick patties. Place remaining ½ cup bread crumbs in a shallow dish. Carefully brush both sides of each patty with oil. Dip patties into bread crumbs, turning to coat both sides.

3. Preheat a grill pan or large skillet over medium heat. Add patties to pan or skillet. Cook for 10 to 12 minutes or until heated through, turning patties once halfway through cooking. (Reduce heat to medium-low if patties brown too quickly.)

4. Spread one side of bread slices with salad dressing. Top with spinach, patties, and tomato. **Makes 4 burgers.**

Barbecued Pork Sandwiches

Making your own barbecue sauce, rather than using a purchased sauce, reduces the sodium content in this recipe. If you're short on time, make the sauce ahead and store it in the refrigerator for up to 3 days.

PER SANDWICH: 208 cal., 2 g total fat (0 g sat. fat), 37 mg chol., 365 mg sodium, 29 g carb., 3 g fiber, 17 g pro. Exchanges: 0.5 vegetable, 1.5 starch, 2 lean meat. Carb choices: 2.

- **Nonstick cooking spray**
- **⅔ cup chopped onion**
- **2 cloves garlic, minced**
- **⅔ cup water**
- **½ of a 6-ounce can (⅓ cup) tomato paste**
- **2 tablespoons red wine vinegar**
- **1 tablespoon packed brown sugar or brown sugar substitute* equivalent to 1 tablespoon sugar**
- **1½ teaspoons chili powder**
- **1 teaspoon dried oregano, crushed**
- **1 teaspoon Worcestershire sauce**
- **12 ounces pork tenderloin**
- **1 medium green sweet pepper, cut into thin strips**
- **6 whole wheat hamburger buns, split and toasted**

1. For sauce, lightly coat an unheated small saucepan with nonstick cooking spray. Preheat saucepan over medium heat. Add onion and garlic; cook and stir about 5 minutes or until onion is tender. Stir in the water, tomato paste, vinegar, brown sugar, chili powder, oregano, and Worcestershire sauce. Bring to boiling; reduce heat. Simmer, uncovered, about 10 minutes or until desired consistency, stirring occasionally.

2. Meanwhile, trim fat from meat. Cut meat into bite-size strips. Lightly coat an unheated large skillet with cooking spray. Preheat skillet over medium-high heat. Add meat; sprinkle with ¼ teaspoon *salt*. Cook and stir for 2 to 3 minutes or until meat is slightly pink in center. Stir in the sauce and sweet pepper; heat through. Serve the meat mixture in toasted buns. **Makes 6 sandwiches.**

***Sugar Substitutes:** Choose from Sweet'N Low Brown or Sugar Twin Granulated Brown. Follow package directions to use product amount equivalent to 1 tablespoon sugar.

PER SERVING WITH SUBSTITUTE: same as above, except 199 cal., 27 g carb.

Barbecued Pork Sandwiches

(grab-and-go sides)

Make your sandwich a real meal. To round it out, add one of these easy-to-grab sides.

1. **Add** a handful of packaged baby carrots, or cut regular carrots into julienne sticks.
2. **Halve, pit, peel, and slice** an avocado.
3. **Peel and cut** julienne sticks of crunchy jicama.
4. **Grab** a handful of cherry or grape tomatoes.
5. **Try** a couple of pieces of pickled vegetables such as asparagus or green beans.
6. **Go** for a few slices of dill pickle.
7. **Cut** a wedge of iceberg lettuce and add a drizzle of bottled low-carb salad dressing.
8. **Pack** in some raw broccoli, a nutrition powerhouse.
9. **Cook** a few protein-rich fresh or frozen sweet soybeans (edamame).
10. **Limit** yourself to one serving of baked potato chips.

Mexi-Pork Wraps

Italian-Style Sloppy Joes

Mexi-Pork Wraps

An anchor of refried beans helps hug the pork strips and fresh vegetable filling to the tortilla.

PER WRAP: 280 cal., 9 g total fat (2 g sat. fat), 39 mg chol., 419 mg sodium, 26 g carb., 12 g fiber, 23 g pro. Exchanges: 0.5 vegetable, 1.5 starch, 2.5 lean meat, 1 fat. Carb choices: 2.

1 tablespoon olive oil
8 ounces lean boneless pork, cut into thin bite-size strips
1 clove garlic, minced
½ cup frozen whole kernel corn, thawed
½ cup chopped bottled roasted red sweet peppers
¼ cup sliced green onions
3 tablespoons lime juice
½ teaspoon ground cumin
⅛ teaspoon cayenne pepper (optional)
½ cup canned refried black beans*
4 8-inch whole grain flour tortillas
½ cup shredded romaine lettuce
½ cup chopped tomatoes
Light dairy sour cream (optional)

1. In a large skillet, heat oil over medium-high heat. Add pork and garlic; cook for 4 to 5 minutes or until pork is cooked through and juices run clear. Set aside.

2. In a medium bowl, stir together corn, roasted red peppers, green onions, 2 tablespoons of the lime juice, the cumin, and, if desired, cayenne pepper. In a small bowl, stir together refried black beans and the remaining 1 tablespoon lime juice.

3. Spread 2 tablespoons of the black bean mixture in a 2-inch-wide strip down the center of each tortilla. Top with pork strips, corn mixture, romaine, and tomatoes. Fold bottom edge of each tortilla up and over the filling. Roll tortillas around filling. If desired, serve wraps with sour cream. **Makes 4 wraps.**

***Test Kitchen Tip:** If you can't find refried black beans, rinse and drain half of a 15-ounce can black beans. In a small bowl, mash beans; stir in 1 tablespoon lime juice.

Mexi-Chicken Wraps: Prepare as above, except substitute skinless, boneless chicken breast halves, cut into bite-size strips, for the pork.

PER WRAP: 270 cal., 8 g total fat (2 g sat. fat), 33 mg chol., 423 mg sodium, 26 g carb., 12 g fiber, 23 g pro. Exchanges: 0.5 vegetable, 1.5 starch, 2.5 lean meat. Carb choices: 2.

Italian-Style Sloppy Joes

To toast buns, place them, cut sides up, on a broiler pan, then broil them about 4 inches from the heat for 1 to 2 minutes or until golden.

PER SANDWICH: 281 cal., 10 g total fat (5 g sat. fat), 50 mg chol., 583 mg sodium, 25 g carb., 3 g fiber, 20 g pro. Exchanges: 1.5 starch, 2.5 lean meat, 1 fat. Carb choices: 1.5.

12 ounces 90% or higher lean ground beef
½ cup chopped onion
1 8-ounce can tomato sauce
¼ teaspoon dried oregano, crushed
¼ teaspoon dried basil, crushed
6 whole wheat or white hamburger buns, split and toasted
½ cup shredded reduced-fat mozzarella cheese (2 ounces)
¼ cup finely shredded Parmesan cheese (1 ounce)

1. In a large skillet, cook ground beef and onion until meat is brown and onion is tender. Drain off fat. Stir in tomato sauce, oregano, and basil. Bring mixture to boiling; reduce heat. Cover and simmer for 15 minutes. Divide beef mixture among hamburger bun bottoms; sprinkle with mozzarella and Parmesan cheeses. Add bun tops. **Makes 6 sandwiches.**

Beef and Cabbage Wraps

To get everyone involved in the kitchen, set out the tortillas, filling, and condiments and let diners assemble their own wraps.

PER WRAP: 356 cal., 12 g total fat (5 g sat. fat), 55 mg chol., 561 mg sodium, 33 g carb., 12 g fiber, 27 g pro. Exchanges: 0.5 vegetable, 2 starch, 3 lean meat, 1 fat. Carb choices: 2.

- **4 8-inch whole wheat or regular flour tortillas**
- **12 ounces 90% or higher lean ground beef**
- **½ cup chopped onion**
- **1 cup frozen whole kernel corn**
- **¼ cup bottled barbecue sauce**
- **2 cups packaged shredded cabbage with carrot (coleslaw mix)**
- **Bottled barbecue sauce (optional)**

1. Wrap tortillas tightly in foil. Heat in a 350°F oven about 10 minutes or until heated through

2. Meanwhile, for filling, in a large skillet, cook meat and onion until meat is brown and onion is tender. Drain off fat. Stir corn and the ¼ cup barbecue sauce into mixture. Cook and stir until heated through.

3. To serve, spoon about ⅓ cup of the filling below center of each tortilla. Top with cabbage with carrot. Roll up from bottom. If desired, serve with additional barbecue sauce. **Makes 4 wraps.**

Beef and Cabbage Wraps

Grilled Steak Fajitas

Let your grill do the work—the vegetables, steak, and tortillas all cook over the fire.

PER SERVING: 333 cal., 12 g total fat (3 g sat. fat), 69 mg chol., 454 mg sodium, 22 g carb., 12 g fiber, 33 g pro. Exchanges: 1 vegetable, 1 starch, 4 lean meat. Carb choices: 1.5.

- **3 green and/or red sweet peppers, sliced**
- **1 medium onion, sliced**
- **1 tablespoon olive oil**
- **1½ teaspoons fajita seasoning**
- **1 clove garlic, minced**
- **1 pound boneless beef top sirloin steak, cut 1 inch thick**
- **4 8-inch whole wheat flour tortillas**
- **Purchased salsa (optional)**
- **Light dairy sour cream (optional)**

1. Fold a 36×18-inch piece of heavy foil in half crosswise. Place sweet peppers and onion in the center of the foil. Drizzle with oil; sprinkle with ½ teaspoon of the fajita seasoning and the garlic. Bring up the opposite edges of the foil; seal with a double fold. Fold in remaining edges, leaving space for steam to build. Set aside.

2. Sprinkle the remaining 1 teaspoon fajita seasoning on both sides of steak; rub in with your fingers. For a charcoal grill, place steak and the vegetable packet on the grill rack directly over medium coals. Grill steak, uncovered, until desired doneness, turning once halfway through grilling. Allow 14 to 18 minutes for medium-rare doneness (145°F) or 18 to 22 minutes for medium doneness (160°F). Remove steak and keep warm. Grill vegetables about 20 minutes or until tender. (For a gas grill, preheat grill. Reduce heat to medium. Place steak and vegetable packet on grill rack over heat. Cover and grill as above.)

3. Meanwhile, wrap tortillas in foil. Place tortilla packet next to steak on grill rack; grill about 10 minutes or until tortillas are heated through. Slice meat into thin bite-size strips. Divide meat among tortillas; top with vegetables. Roll up. If desired, serve with salsa and sour cream. **Makes 4 servings.**

Quick Tip:

Add colorful goodness to your fajitas. Even though red and green are the most common colors of sweet peppers, you can also throw yellow, orange, and even purple sweet peppers into the mix. All sweet peppers are loaded with vitamins A and C as well as many other vitamins and nutrients.

Grilled Steak Fajitas

Chicken and Black Bean Wraps

Serve leftover Black Bean-Smoked Chile Dip with baked tortilla chips as a snack.

PER WRAP: 324 cal., 8 g total fat (2 g sat. fat), 72 mg chol., 600 mg sodium, 24 g carb., 14 g fiber, 38 g pro. Exchanges: 1 vegetable, 1.5 starch, 4.5 very lean meat, 1 fat. Carb choices: 1.5

- **½ cup Black Bean-Smoked Chile Dip (see recipe, right)**
- **4 7- or 8-inch whole wheat flour tortillas**
- **12 ounces cooked skinless chicken or turkey breast, shredded and chopped (about 2⅓ cups)**
- **4 cups shredded or torn romaine lettuce or whole fresh baby spinach leaves**
- **1 cup coarsely snipped fresh cilantro**
- **¼ cup purchased salsa**

1. Spread Black Bean-Smoked Chile Dip on one side of each tortilla. Top with chicken, romaine, cilantro, and salsa. Fold bottom edge of each tortilla up and over the filling. Roll tortillas around filling. If desired, secure with toothpicks. **Makes 4 wraps.**

Chicken and Black Bean Wraps

Black Bean-Smoked Chile Dip: In a small saucepan, heat 1 tablespoon canola oil over medium heat. Add ¾ cup finely chopped onion, 1 teaspoon ground coriander, and 1 teaspoon ground cumin; cover and cook about 10 minutes or until very tender, stirring occasionally. Remove from heat; stir in ¼ cup snipped fresh cilantro. Transfer onion mixture to a blender or food processor. Add one 15-ounce can black beans, rinsed and drained; ½ cup water; 1 tablespoon lime juice; 1 teaspoon finely chopped chipotle chile pepper in adobo sauce;* and ⅛ teaspoon salt. Cover and blend or process until nearly smooth. Serve immediately or cover and chill for up to 3 days before serving. **Makes 1⅔ cups.**

***Test Kitchen Tip:** Because chile peppers contain volatile oils that can burn your skin and eyes, avoid direct contact with them as much as possible. When working with chile peppers, wear plastic or rubber gloves. If your bare hands do touch the peppers, wash your hands and nails well with soap and warm water.

Chicken Focaccia Sandwiches

An opened jar of roasted red sweet peppers will store in the refrigerator for up to two weeks. Put the peppers to good use by adding them to an omelet or salad.

PER SANDWICH: 246 cal., 7 g total fat (1 g sat. fat), 49 mg chol., 335 mg sodium, 27 g carb., 0 g fiber, 20 g pro. Exchanges: 2 starch, 2 lean meat. Carb choices: 2.

- **1 8-inch tomato or onion Italian flatbread (focaccia) or 12 slices whole grain bread***
- **⅓ cup light mayonnaise or salad dressing**
- **1 cup lightly packed fresh basil leaves**
- **2 cups sliced or shredded cooked chicken breast**
- **½ of a 7-ounce jar roasted red sweet peppers, drained and cut into strips (about ½ cup)**

1. If using focaccia bread, use a long serrated knife to split in half horizontally. Spread cut sides of bread halves with mayonnaise. Layer basil leaves, chicken, and roasted sweet peppers between bread halves. Cut into wedges. **Makes 6 sandwiches.**

***Test Kitchen Tip:** If using the whole grain bread, toast bread and spread mayonnaise on one side of each bread slice. Assemble sandwiches between the spread sides of the bread slices. Cut each sandwich in half to serve.

Quick Tip:

Soft and chewy Italian flatbread, known as focaccia, may vary by bakery. To keep the nutrition numbers in check, look for a loaf that is 8 inches in diameter, then choose your favorite topping—tomato, onion, garlic, herb, or olive.

Chicken Focaccia Sandwich

Chicken Salad Sandwiches

Chicken Salad Sandwiches

Whole wheat bread is the choice for this fruit-studded chicken salad, but German-style pumpernickel or rye bread are good options, too.

PER SANDWICH: 248 cal., 7 g total fat (2 g sat. fat), 86 mg chol., 447 mg sodium, 28 g carb., 5 g fiber, 18 g pro. Exchanges: 1 vegetable, 1.5 starch, 2 very lean meat, 0.5 fat. Carb choices: 2.

1 cup chopped cooked chicken breast (5 ounces)
⅓ cup chopped cored apple or finely chopped celery
1 hard-cooked egg, peeled and chopped
2 tablespoons plain low-fat yogurt
2 tablespoons light mayonnaise or salad dressing
⅛ teaspoon salt
⅛ teaspoon ground black pepper
8 slices whole wheat bread
4 leaf lettuce or romaine lettuce leaves
1 medium tomato, thinly sliced
½ of a small cucumber, thinly sliced (about ¾ cup)

1. In a medium bowl, stir together chicken, apple, and egg. Add yogurt, mayonnaise, salt, and pepper; stir to combine.

2. Top half of the bread slices with a lettuce leaf. Then add tomato slices, cucumber slices, and some of the chicken mixture to each. Top each stack with another bread slice. Cut each sandwich in half to serve. **Makes 4 sandwiches.**

Make-Ahead Directions: If desired, cover and chill the chicken mixture for up to 4 hours before serving.

(pick a pocket)

Pita bread, the Greek version of baked flatbread, is available in white or whole wheat. Although it is most commonly known for its pocket, it comes pocketless as well. Because a pita pocket is low in fat and similar in carbohydrates to a slice of loaf-style bread, it makes a great bread option for people with diabetes or those dieting. To create easy-to-eat, grab-and-go-style sandwiches, fill the pocket with meats, cheeses, salads, hummus, veggies, and more. The soft, nonpocket version, also known as restaurant-style, is perfect for grilling and serving alongside a salad.

Chicken and Hummus Pitas

Delectable served warm, this pocket sandwich is also great to chill and tote for lunch.

PER SERVING: 289 cal., 10 g total fat (2 g sat. fat), 34 mg chol., 380 mg sodium, 31 g carb., 5 g fiber, 20 g pro. Exchanges: 1.5 starch, 0.5 carb., 2 very lean meat, 1 fat. Carb choices: 2.

1 tablespoon olive oil
1 teaspoon lemon juice
¼ teaspoon paprika
Dash salt
Dash ground black pepper
2 medium skinless, boneless chicken breast halves (8 to 12 ounces total)
2 large whole wheat pita bread rounds, halved crosswise
1 7-ounce carton hummus
¾ cup coarsely chopped roma tomatoes
½ cup thinly sliced cucumber
⅓ cup plain low-fat yogurt

1. Preheat broiler. In a small bowl, combine oil, lemon juice, paprika, salt, and pepper. Place chicken on the unheated rack of a broiler pan. Brush all sides of the chicken breast halves with the oil mixture. Broil 4 to 5 inches from heat for 12 to 15 minutes or until chicken is no longer pink (170°F), turning once halfway through broiling. Cool slightly; cut into strips.

2. Open pita halves to create four pockets. Spread hummus inside pita pockets. Stuff pockets with chicken strips, tomatoes, cucumber, and yogurt. **Makes 4 servings.**

Chicken and Hummus Pitas

Turkey-Tomato Wraps

Turkey-Tomato Wraps

Hummus comes plain and in a variety of flavors. If you opt for a flavor, choose roasted red pepper or Greek-style; their sodium content is similar to that of the original.

PER WRAP: 233 cal., 6 g total fat (1 g sat. fat), 19 mg chol., 559 mg sodium, 34 g carb., 5 g fiber, 15 g pro. Exchanges: 1 vegetable, 2 starch, 1.5 lean meat. Carb choices: 2.

1 7-ounce carton hummus
4 7- to 8-inch tomato-basil or whole wheat flour tortillas
6 ounces thinly sliced cooked peppered turkey breast
4 romaine lettuce leaves, ribs removed
3 small tomatoes, thinly sliced
3 thin slices red onion, separated into rings

1. Spread hummus evenly over tortillas. Layer turkey, romaine leaves, tomatoes, and red onion near one edge. Roll up tortillas, starting from the edge with the turkey. Cut into quarters to serve. **Makes 4 wraps.**

Thai Chicken-Broccoli Wraps

If chicken breast strips for stir-frying are unavailable, use skinless, boneless chicken breast halves and cut your own bite-size strips.

PER WRAP: 312 cal., 11 g total fat (3 g sat. fat), 49 mg chol., 565 mg sodium, 21 g carb., 12 g fiber, 32 g pro. Exchanges: 0.5 vegetable, 1 starch, 4 lean meat, 1 fat. Carb choices: 1.5.

12 ounces skinless, boneless chicken breast strips for stir-frying
¼ teaspoon garlic powder
⅛ teaspoon black pepper
Nonstick cooking spray
2 cups packaged shredded broccoli (broccoli slaw mix)
¼ teaspoon ground ginger
4 7- to 8-inch whole wheat flour tortillas, warmed*
1 recipe Peanut Sauce (see recipe, below)

1. Sprinkle chicken strips with garlic powder and pepper. Coat an unheated large nonstick skillet with nonstick cooking spray. Preheat skillet over medium-high heat. Add seasoned chicken; cook and stir for 2 to 3 minutes or until chicken is no longer pink. Remove chicken from skillet; keep warm. Add broccoli and ginger to skillet. Cook and stir for 2 to 3 minutes or until vegetables are crisp-tender.

2. Spread tortillas with Peanut Sauce. Top with chicken strips and vegetable mixture. Roll up tortillas. Serve immediately. **Makes 4 wraps.**

Peanut Sauce: In a small saucepan, combine 3 tablespoons creamy peanut butter; 2 tablespoons water; 1 tablespoon reduced-sodium soy sauce; 1 clove garlic, minced; and ¼ teaspoon ground ginger. Heat over very low heat until melted and smooth, whisking constantly.

***Test Kitchen Tip:** To warm tortillas, preheat oven to 350°F. Wrap tortillas tightly in foil. Heat in the oven about 10 minutes or until heated through.

Pulled Chicken Sandwiches

Here's a Southern-style classic, complete with pickle and onion.

PER SANDWICH: 254 cal., 8 g total fat (2 g sat. fat), 42 mg chol., 539 mg sodium, 27 g carb., 1 g fiber, 19 g pro. Exchanges: 2 starch, 2 lean meat. Carb choices: 2.

1 recipe Barbecue Sauce (see recipe, right)
2 cups shredded cooked chicken breast
6 whole wheat hamburger buns, split and, if desired, toasted
Red onion slices (optional)
Dill pickle slices (optional)

1. Prepare Barbecue Sauce. Add shredded chicken to sauce. Heat through, stirring frequently. Serve on split buns. If desired, serve with red onion slices and dill pickle slices. **Makes 6 sandwiches.**

Barbecue Sauce: In a medium saucepan, heat 1 tablespoon olive oil over medium heat. Add 1/4 cup finely chopped onion; cook for 3 to 5 minutes or until tender, stirring occasionally. Add one 8-ounce can tomato sauce, 2 tablespoons tomato paste, 1 tablespoon Dijon-style mustard, 1 tablespoon Worcestershire sauce, and 1 teaspoon honey. Bring to boiling; reduce heat. Simmer, uncovered, about 5 minutes or until desired consistency. Season to taste with ground black pepper.

simple sides and salads

Italian Pasta Salad

Filling your plate with colorful foods is usually a good thing — veggies, greens, and fruits are loaded with vitamins and other healthful nutrients. Pick one of these vibrant recipes to round out your meal, choosing fat and carb numbers that fit your daily meal plan.

Italian Pasta Salad

Toss this summertime staple together while your favorite cut of meat is sizzling on the grill.

PER SERVING: 123 cal., 5 g total fat (1 g sat. fat), 0 mg chol., 81 mg sodium, 16 g carb., 2 g fiber, 3 g pro. Exchanges: 1 starch, 1 fat. Carb choices: 1.

4 ounces dried whole wheat rotini, penne, or bow tie pasta (about 1½ cups)
1 cup fresh sugar snap peas, trimmed
½ cup chopped red sweet pepper
¼ cup shredded fresh basil*
2 tablespoons pitted kalamata or niçoise olives, quartered
2 tablespoons red wine vinegar
2 tablespoons olive oil
1 clove garlic, minced
⅛ teaspoon salt
Dash ground black pepper

1. Cook pasta according to package directions, adding the sugar snap peas for the last 1 minute of cooking. Drain well. Rinse with cold water; drain again. In a large bowl, combine pasta mixture, sweet pepper, basil, and olives. Set aside.

2. For dressing, in a screw-top jar, combine red wine vinegar, oil, garlic, salt, and black pepper. Cover and shake well. Pour dressing over pasta and vegetables; toss gently to coat. **Makes 6 (½-cup) servings.**

***Test Kitchen Tip:** To shred (chiffonade) fresh basil, stack several leaves and roll up the leaves. Starting at one end, use a sharp knife to cut crosswise into thin slices.

Minted Wild Rice and Barley Salad

Minted Wild Rice and Barley Salad

Golden raisins bring hints of sweetness as well as nuggets of color to this multigrain combo, but regular raisins are a fine substitute.

PER SERVING: 136 cal., 3 g total fat (0 g sat. fat), 0 mg chol., 103 mg sodium, 26 g carb., 3 g fiber, 4 g pro. Exchanges: 0.5 fruit, 1 starch, 0.5 fat. Carb choices: 2.

½ cup wild rice, rinsed and drained
¼ cup barley
1 cup fresh pea pods, cut into thirds
⅓ cup golden raisins
3 green onions, sliced
1 teaspoon finely shredded orange peel
⅓ cup orange juice
1 tablespoon olive oil
¼ teaspoon salt
⅛ teaspoon ground black pepper
2 tablespoons snipped fresh mint
Shredded orange peel (optional)

1. In a medium saucepan, bring 2 cups *water* to boiling; stir in uncooked wild rice and barley. Return to boiling; reduce heat. Cover and simmer about 40 minutes or until wild rice and barley are tender. Drain off liquid. Transfer wild rice and barley to a large bowl.

2. Stir in pea pods, raisins, green onions, the 1 teaspoon orange peel, the orange juice, oil, salt, and pepper. Cover and chill for 4 to 6 hours.

3. Stir in mint. If desired, garnish with additional orange peel. **Makes 6 (about ⅔-cup) servings.**

Whole Wheat Orzo Pilaf with Mushrooms

Just a few pine nuts add a lot of flavor but not many calories or carbs.

PER SERVING: 148 cal., 4 g total fat (0 g sat. fat), 0 mg chol., 160 mg sodium, 23 g carb., 5 g fiber, 6 g pro. Exchanges: 0.5 vegetable, 0.5 starch, 0.5 fat. Carb choices: 1.5

2 teaspoons olive oil
8 ounces fresh button, shiitake, portobello and/or cremini mushrooms, sliced
1 medium onion, chopped
1 14-ounce can reduced-sodium chicken broth
1 cup dried whole wheat orzo
2 tablespoons pine nuts, toasted
2 tablespoons snipped fresh parsley

1. In a large saucepan, heat oil over medium heat. Add mushrooms and onion; cook about 10 minutes or until vegetables are tender, stirring occasionally.

2. Add broth to mushroom mixture; bring to boiling. Stir in orzo; reduce heat. Cover and simmer about 15 minutes or until orzo is tender and most of the liquid is absorbed, stirring occasionally. Remove from heat. Stir in pine nuts and parsley. Serve warm. **Makes 6 (½-cup) servings.**

Couscous with Orange

Try this made-in-a-flash side served with grilled poultry.

PER SERVING: 108 cal., 0 g total fat, 0 mg chol., 96 mg sodium, 23 g carb., 4 g fiber, 4 g pro. Exchanges: 1.5 starch. Carb choices: 1.5.

1 cup reduced-sodium chicken broth
⅛ teaspoon ground black pepper
⅔ cup whole wheat quick-cooking couscous
2 green onions, chopped
1 teaspoon finely shredded orange peel
1 medium orange, peeled, sectioned, and coarsely chopped

1. In a medium saucepan, combine chicken broth and pepper; bring to boiling. Stir in couscous and green onions; remove from heat. Cover and let stand for 5 minutes. Fluff couscous with a fork; gently stir in the orange peel and chopped orange. Serve immediately. **Makes 6 (about ½-cup) servings.**

Couscous with Orange

(take two on tabbouleh)

Tabbouleh is a Middle Eastern salad, or meze, that is typically made with bulgur wheat, chopped tomatoes, cucumber, parsley, olive oil, and lemon juice. Here, it takes on new flavor when the chewy bulgur's combined with pungent cilantro, tart dried cranberries, and zesty lime. Try it spooned into a whole wheat pita pocket and sprinkled with a little crumbled feta. A handful of shredded cooked chicken or cubes of cooked lean pork turns this refreshing side into a main dish when it's served over fresh baby spinach.

Cilantro Tabbouleh with Cranberries

Cilantro Tabbouleh with Cranberries

The bran on the bulgur gives this dish a wonderful chewiness and adds healthful fiber.

PER SERVING: 82 cal., 0 g total fat (0 g sat. fat), 0 mg chol., 184 mg sodium, 18 g carb., 4 g fiber, 3 g pro. Exchanges: 1 starch. Carb choices: 1.

Nonstick cooking spray
1 tablespoon finely chopped shallot or onion
1¼ cups reduced-sodium chicken broth
½ cup bulgur
½ cup chopped seeded cucumber
2 tablespoons snipped fresh cilantro
2 tablespoons dried cranberries
¼ teaspoon finely shredded lime peel
1 tablespoon lime juice
Dash ground black pepper

1. Coat an unheated small nonstick saucepan with nonstick cooking spray. Preheat saucepan over medium heat. Add shallot to hot saucepan; cook and stir about 3 minutes or just until tender. Add chicken broth; bring to boiling. Stir in uncooked bulgur. Return to boiling; reduce heat. Cover and simmer about 15 minutes or until tender. Remove from heat; cool slightly. Transfer cooked bulgur to a large bowl. Cover and chill about 3 hours or until completely cool.

2. Add cucumber, cilantro, cranberries, lime peel, lime juice, and pepper to cooled bulgur; mix well. **Makes 4 (½-cup) servings.**

Make-Ahead Directions: Prepare as above. Cover and chill for up to 24 hours.

Jicama Coleslaw

Coleslaw goes uptown with peach, jicama, and cilantro added to the cabbage and a tangy apple juice vinaigrette instead of the usual creamy dressing.

PER SERVING: 77 cal., 4 g total fat (0 g sat. fat), 0 mg chol., 84 mg sodium, 12 g carb., 2 g fiber, 1 g pro. Exchanges: 0.5 vegetable, 0.5 fruit, 1 fat. Carb choices: 1.

2 cups shredded red or green cabbage
⅔ cup thin bite-size strips peeled jicama
1 medium peach (peeled if desired) or nectarine, pitted and chopped, or 1 medium apple, cored and chopped
3 tablespoons thinly sliced green onions
2 tablespoons snipped fresh cilantro or flat-leaf parsley

Jicama Coleslaw

2 tablespoons apple juice or apple cider
1 tablespoon cider vinegar
1 tablespoon salad oil
⅛ teaspoon salt
⅛ teaspoon ground black pepper

1. In a very large bowl, combine cabbage, jicama, peach, green onions, and cilantro.

2. For dressing, in a small bowl, whisk together apple juice, cider vinegar, oil, salt, and pepper. Pour dressing over cabbage mixture; toss to coat. Cover and chill for 2 to 4 hours. **Makes 4 servings.**

Make-Ahead Directions: Prepare as above, except do not add peach, nectarine, or apple. Cover and chill for up to 24 hours. To serve, stir in peach, nectarine, or apple.

Asian Coleslaw

(potluck pointers)

Having diabetes shouldn't prevent you from enjoying an old-fashioned picnic potluck. Use these helpful tips:

1. **Plan ahead** how much from each food exchange group you can eat at the gathering.
2. **Keep an eye on portions.** Spoon up smaller portions than normal—you'll eat more variety than at home.
3. **Start with veggies.** Nibbling on non-starchy vegetables before the meal will help you feel full faster so you'll eat less overall.
4. **Control the carbs.** Be reasonable about corn on the cob, potato or pasta salad, sweets, and high-calorie beverages.
5. **Choose lean meats.** Skinless chicken breast, fish, pork loin, or lean turkey are good bets.
6. **Drink plenty of water** to stay well hydrated and avoid high-calorie beverages.
7. **Be discerning about desserts.** Seasonal fruits are good choices.
8. **Avoid nonstop noshing**. Goodies may tempt you all day, but stick to your meal plan. Bring your own snacks.
9. **Eat safely.** Make sure hot foods stay hot (above 140°F) and cold foods stay cold (below 40°F).
10. **Check your blood glucose** if you're more active than normal or veering from your meal plan.

Grilled Corn Salad

Asian Coleslaw

Do you like fish tacos? Use some of this crunchy salad as a condiment the next time you make them.

PER SERVING: 68 cal., 3 g total fat (1 g sat. fat), 0 mg chol., 207 mg sodium, 9 g carb., 1 g fiber, 1 g pro. Exchanges: 1.5 vegetable, 0.5 fat. Carb choices: 0.5.

- **4 cups packaged shredded cabbage with carrot (coleslaw mix)**
- **1 medium yellow, orange, red, or green sweet pepper, seeded and thinly sliced (1 cup)**
- **¼ cup thinly sliced green onions**
- **¼ cup snipped fresh cilantro**
- **½ cup bottled low-fat sesame ginger salad dressing**

1. In a large bowl, combine coleslaw mix, sweet pepper, green onions, and cilantro. Pour dressing over cabbage mixture; toss gently to coat. Serve immediately or cover and chill up to 24 hours. **Makes 6 (⅔-cup) servings.**

Grilled Corn Salad

Corn, spinach, cherry tomatoes, and fresh oregano make this beguiling salad a home-gardener's delight.

PER SERVING: 107 cal., 4 g total fat (1 g sat. fat), 1 mg chol., 200 mg sodium, 16 g carb., 3 g fiber, 4 g pro. Exchanges: 0.5 vegetable, 1 starch, 0.5 fat. Carb choices: 1.

- **4 ears fresh corn on the cob**
- **½ cup bottled reduced-calorie clear Italian salad dressing**
- **2 cups shredded fresh spinach**
- **2 cups red and/or yellow cherry tomatoes, halved**
- **2 teaspoons snipped fresh oregano or basil**
- **2 tablespoons finely shredded Parmesan cheese**
- **Fresh oregano or basil leaves (optional)**

1. Husk and silk corn. Brush each ear of corn with some of the Italian salad dressing. Place corn on the grill rack directly over medium coals. Grill, uncovered, for 15 to 20 minutes or until tender, turning often. (Or place brushed ears in a shallow baking pan; roast in a 425°F oven for 30 minutes, turning once.) When cool enough to handle, cut kernels from cobs (you should have about 2 cups kernels).

2. In a large bowl, combine corn kernels, spinach, tomatoes, and the 2 teaspoons snipped oregano. Add remaining Italian salad dressing; toss to coat. Spoon corn mixture into six small mugs or bowls. Sprinkle each serving with Parmesan cheese. If desired, garnish with oregano or basil leaves. **Makes 6 (1-cup) servings.**

Greens and Fruit with Mustard Dressing

A little lemon juice prevents the fruit from turning brown.

PER SERVING: 117 cal., 3 g total fat (0 g sat. fat), 0 mg chol., 200 mg sodium, 20 g carb., 3 g fiber, 3 g pro. Exchanges: 1 vegetable, 1 fruit, 0.5 fat. Carb choices: 1.

- **¼ cup plain fat-free yogurt**
- **2 tablespoons Dijon-style mustard**
- **1 tablespoon honey**
- **1½ teaspoons orange juice**
- **1 teaspoon olive oil**
- **1 small Bosc pear, cored and sliced**
- **1 small apple, cored and sliced**
- **1 tablespoon lemon juice**
- **4 cups torn mixed greens**
- **2 tablespoons dry-roasted sunflower kernels**
- **Freshly ground black pepper**

1. For dressing, in a small bowl, whisk together yogurt, mustard, honey, orange juice, and oil until smooth. In a medium bowl, toss pear and apple slices with lemon juice to coat.

2. Place greens on a large serving platter; top with pear and apple slices. Drizzle with dressing. Sprinkle with sunflower kernels and pepper. **Makes 4 (about 1¼-cup) servings.**

Greek Vegetable Salad

Quick Tip:

If you need a cup or two of various veggies and don't want to hassle with cutting them up yourself, purchase them precut from the produce section or the salad bar at your supermarket. Then toss any extra veggies in a salad or stir them into your next pot of soup.

Greek Vegetable Salad

White balsamic vinegar offers a lighter flavor, thinner consistency, and clearer color than the traditional barrel-aged, syrupy brown vinegar.

PER SERVING: 65 cal., 5 g total fat (1 g sat. fat), 3 mg chol., 120 mg sodium, 4 g carb., 1 g fiber, 2 g pro. Exchanges: 1 vegetable, 1 fat. Carb choices: 0.

1 cup chopped tomatoes
½ cup chopped cucumber
¼ cup chopped yellow, red, or green sweet pepper
2 tablespoons chopped red onion
¾ teaspoon snipped fresh thyme or ¼ teaspoon dried thyme, crushed
½ teaspoon snipped fresh oregano or ⅛ teaspoon dried oregano, crushed
1 tablespoon white balsamic vinegar or regular balsamic vinegar
1 tablespoon olive oil
Leaf lettuce (optional)
¼ cup crumbled reduced-fat feta cheese (1 ounce)

1. In a medium bowl, combine tomatoes, cucumber, sweet pepper, red onion, thyme, and oregano. For dressing, in a small bowl, whisk together balsamic vinegar and olive oil. Pour dressing over vegetable mixture. Toss gently to coat.

2. If desired, line a serving bowl with lettuce; spoon in vegetable mixture. Sprinkle with feta cheese. **Makes 4 (½-cup) servings.**

Broccoli and Cauliflower Sauté

Broccoli and Cauliflower Sauté

Low in calories and carbs, these garlicky veggies are a tasty side for broiled or grilled chicken, pork chops, or fish.

PER SERVING: 47 cal., 2 g total fat (0 g sat. fat), 0 mg chol., 88 mg sodium, 4 g carb., 1 g fiber, 1 g pro. Exchanges: 1 vegetable, 0.5 fat. Carb choices: 0.

2 teaspoons olive oil
1 cup broccoli florets
1 cup cauliflower florets
1 clove garlic, thinly sliced
¼ cup dry white wine or reduced-sodium chicken broth
3 tablespoons water
⅛ teaspoon salt
⅛ teaspoon ground black pepper

1. In a large skillet, heat oil over medium-high heat. Add broccoli, cauliflower, and garlic; cook for 2 minutes, stirring occasionally. Carefully add wine, the water, salt, and pepper; reduce heat to low. Cover and cook for 2 minutes. Uncover; raise heat to medium. Cook about 2 minutes or until vegetables are tender, stirring occasionally. **Makes 4 (½-cup) servings.**

Tomato Sauté

You'll love everything about this easy side dish: the fresh tomato flavor, the savory thyme, and the mild mozzarella.

PER SERVING: 88 cal., 6 g total fat (2 g sat. fat), 11 mg chol., 168 mg sodium, 6 g carb., 2 g fiber, 4 g pro. Exchanges: 1 vegetable, 0.5 high fat meat, 0.5 fat. Carb choices: 0.5.

- **2½ cups whole red grape tomatoes, yellow pear tomatoes, and/or cherry tomatoes**
- **2 teaspoons olive oil**
- **¼ cup thinly sliced onion**
- **1 clove garlic, minced**
- **1 teaspoon snipped fresh thyme or ¼ teaspoon dried thyme, crushed**
- **¼ teaspoon salt**
- **¼ teaspoon ground black pepper**
- **2 ounces fresh mozzarella cheese, cut into ½-inch cubes**

1. Halve the tomatoes; set aside. In a large skillet, heat oil over medium heat. Add onion, garlic, and thyme; cook and stir for 2 to 3 minutes or until onion is tender.

2. Add tomatoes, salt, and pepper. Cook and stir for 1 to 2 minutes or until tomatoes are just warmed. Remove from heat. Stir in mozzarella cheese. **Makes 4 (about ½-cup) servings.**

(snap to it)

Inside the edible pods of sugar snap peas hide tender buttons of sweet flavor. Snatch up these crunchy, delicate treats in spring when they're freshest and most affordable. Try them stir-fried, steamed, sautéed, or raw. Served alone or in a veggie combo, they're a treat to eat. They're a healthful choice, too: a half cup of pea pods has only 35 calories and is loaded with iron and vitamins A and C. Store pods for 4 to 7 days in a perforated bag in the refrigerator.

Ginger Vegetable Stir-Fry

For a dynamite meal, roast, broil, or grill your favorite meat or poultry and serve this eye-catching medley of veggies alongside.

PER SERVING: 56 cal., 2 g total fat (0 g sat. fat), 0 mg chol., 120 mg sodium, 7 g carb., 2 g fiber, 2 g pro. Exchanges: 1.5 vegetable, 0.5 fat. Carb choices: 0.5.

½ cup cold water
1 tablespoon reduced-sodium soy sauce
1 teaspoon cornstarch
½ teaspoon ground ginger
1 tablespoon canola oil or cooking oil
2 cups broccoli and/or cauliflower florets
1 large carrot, thinly bias-sliced
¼ cup chopped onion
1 clove garlic, minced
½ cup fresh sugar snap peas, tips and strings removed
½ of a large red or green sweet pepper, seeded and cut into strips
½ of a 14-ounce can baby corn, drained and halved crosswise
½ of an 8-ounce can sliced water chestnuts, drained

1. In a small bowl, stir together the water, soy sauce, cornstarch, and ginger; set aside.

2. In a wok or large skillet, heat oil over medium-high heat. Add broccoli and/or cauliflower, carrot, onion, and garlic; stir-fry for 6 to 8 minutes or just until tender. Add sugar snap peas, sweet pepper, baby corn, and water chestnuts; stir-fry for 2 minutes.

3. Stir cornstarch mixture; add to vegetables in wok or skillet. Cook and stir until thickened and bubbly. Cook and stir for 2 minutes more. **Makes 6 (⅔-cup) servings.**

Ginger Vegetable Stir-Fry

eye-opening breakfasts

Southwest Skillet

Whether you're on the run or have time to lounge, make the morning meal first on your to-do list. Start your day with one of these healthful beginnings—hearty whole-grain cereals, sizzling egg skillets, chill-and-bake breakfast casseroles, fresh-baked breads, and more.

Southwest Skillet

Watch the almonds closely because once the toasting process starts, they brown quickly.

PER SERVING: 157 cal., 10 g total fat (2 g sat. fat), 212 mg chol., 230 mg sodium, 9 g carb., 3 g fiber, 9 g pro. Exchanges: 1 vegetable, 1 medium-fat meat, 1 fat. Carb choices: 0.5.

2 tablespoons sliced almonds
1 yellow sweet pepper, seeded and cut into thin bite-size strips
1 fresh jalapeño chile pepper, seeded and chopped*
1 tablespoon olive oil or cooking oil
4 medium tomatoes, seeded and chopped (about 3 cups)
1 teaspoon chili powder
½ teaspoon ground cumin
¼ teaspoon salt
4 eggs
1 medium ripe avocado, halved, pitted, peeled, and coarsely chopped (optional)

1. In a large skillet, toast almonds over medium heat for 4 to 5 minutes or until light brown, stirring occasionally. Remove almonds from skillet; set aside. In the same skillet, cook and stir sweet pepper and jalapeño pepper in hot oil about 2 minutes or until tender. Stir in tomatoes, chili powder, cumin, and salt. Cook, uncovered, for 5 minutes, stirring occasionally.

2. Break 1 of the eggs into a measuring cup. Carefully slide egg onto tomato mixture. Repeat with remaining eggs, spacing eggs as evenly as possible.

3. Cover and simmer over medium-low heat for 3 to 5 minutes or until the egg whites are completely set and yolks begin to thicken but are not hard. If desired, top with avocado. Sprinkle with the toasted almonds. **Makes 4 servings.**

***Test Kitchen Tip:** Because chile peppers contain volatile oils that can burn your skin and eyes, wear plastic or rubber gloves when working with them. If your bare hands do touch the peppers, wash your hands and nails well with soap and warm water.

Quick Tip:

Herbes de Provence is a blend of dried herbs that grow in abundance in the Provence region of southern France. Basil, thyme, sage, rosemary, summer savory, marjoram, fennel seeds, and/or lavender make up this savory combination. Try the herb mix as a rub on beef steak, lamb chops, and pork loin.

Mushroom Omelets

Mushroom Omelets

Double or triple this upscale recipe to serve guests at a weekend or holiday brunch.

PER SERVING: 168 cal., 6 g total fat (3 g sat. fat), 13 mg chol., 512 mg sodium, 10 g carb., 2 g fiber, 20 g pro. Exchanges: 1.5 vegetable, 2.5 lean meat, 0.5 fat. Carb choices: 0.5.

Nonstick cooking spray
2 cups sliced fresh mushrooms
3 tablespoons sliced green onions
1 clove garlic, minced
1 cup refrigerated or frozen egg product, thawed, or 4 eggs, lightly beaten
¼ teaspoon herbes de Provence or dried thyme or basil, crushed
⅛ teaspoon salt
Dash ground black pepper
1 teaspoon olive oil
¼ cup shredded part-skim mozzarella cheese (1 ounce)
1 medium roma tomato, chopped
1 tablespoon finely shredded Asiago or Parmesan cheese
Fresh basil or parsley leaves (optional)

1. Lightly coat an unheated 6- to 7-inch nonstick skillet with flared side with nonstick cooking spray. Preheat skillet over medium heat. Add mushrooms, green onions, and garlic; cook and stir until mushrooms are tender. Using a slotted spoon, remove mushroom mixture from skillet; set aside. If necessary, drain skillet; carefully wipe out skillet with paper towels.

2. In a medium bowl, combine eggs, herbes de Provence, salt, and pepper.

3. Add half of the oil to the skillet; heat skillet over medium heat. Pour half of the egg mixture into skillet. Using a wooden or plastic spatula, immediately begin stirring the eggs gently but continuously until mixture resembles small pieces of cooked egg surrounded by liquid egg. Stop stirring. Cook for 30 to 60 seconds more or until egg mixture is set and shiny.

4. Sprinkle with half of the mozzarella cheese. Top with half of the mushroom mixture. Continue cooking until cheese just begins to melt. Using the spatula, lift and fold an edge of the omelet partially over filling. Remove from skillet; cover and keep warm.

5. Repeat with remaining oil, egg mixture, mozzarella cheese, and mushroom mixture. Top omelets with tomato, Asiago cheese, and, if desired, fresh basil. **Makes 2 servings.**

Breakfast Bake

Boost the fresh-flavor factor with 1 tablespoon snipped fresh chives stirred into the egg mixture.

PER SERVING: 198 cal., 9 g total fat (3 g sat. fat), 228 mg chol., 547 mg sodium, 15 g carb., 2 g fiber, 16 g pro. Exchanges: 1 starch, 2 lean meat. Carb choices: 1.

Nonstick cooking spray
4 slices whole wheat bread
½ cup diced cooked lean ham (about 2¼ ounces)
⅓ cup shredded reduced-fat cheddar cheese
4 eggs
⅔ cup fat-free milk
¼ teaspoon ground black pepper

1. Lightly coat two 16- to 20-ounce casseroles with nonstick cooking spray. Tear bread into bite-size pieces. Divide bread among prepared casseroles. Sprinkle with ham and cheese.

2. In a medium bowl, combine eggs, milk, and pepper. Beat with a rotary beater or wire whisk. Pour egg mixture evenly over bread; press lightly with the back of a spoon to thoroughly moisten bread. Cover and chill for 2 to 24 hours.

3. Preheat oven to 325°F. Bake casseroles, uncovered, for 30 to 35 minutes or until a knife inserted near centers comes out clean. Let stand for 10 minutes before serving. **Makes 4 servings (½ casserole per serving).**

Egg and Potato Casserole

Egg and Potato Casserole

Take your choice of frozen broccoli or asparagus for this hearty breakfast bake.

PER SERVING: 142 cal., 3 g total fat (2 g sat. fat), 12 mg chol., 354 mg sodium, 14 g carb., 1 g fiber, 15 g pro. Exchanges: 0.5 vegetable, 1 starch, 1.5 lean meat. Carb choices: 1.

Nonstick cooking spray
- **⅔ cup frozen diced hash brown potatoes with onions and peppers**
- **⅓ cup frozen cut broccoli and/or frozen cut asparagus**
- **2 tablespoons chopped Canadian-style bacon or cooked lean ham**
- **2 tablespoons evaporated fat-free milk**
- **2 teaspoons all-purpose flour**
- **⅔ cup refrigerated or frozen egg product, thawed**
- **3 tablespoons shredded reduced-fat cheddar cheese**
- **1 teaspoon snipped fresh basil or ¼ teaspoon dried basil, crushed**
- **⅛ teaspoon ground black pepper**

1. Preheat oven to 350°F. Lightly coat two 10-ounce casseroles or quiche dishes with nonstick cooking spray. Arrange hash brown potatoes and broccoli in bottoms of casseroles; top with Canadian bacon. In a small bowl, gradually stir milk into flour. Stir in egg, half of the cheese, the basil, and black pepper. Pour egg mixture over vegetables.

2. Bake, uncovered, for 25 to 30 minutes or until a knife inserted near centers comes out clean. Sprinkle with the remaining cheese. Let stand for 5 minutes before serving. **Makes 2 servings.**

Zucchini Pancakes

These savory little cakes are perfect for brunch.

PER PANCAKE: 69 cal., 3 g total fat (1 g sat. fat), 3 mg chol., 154 mg sodium, 7 g carb., 1 g fiber, 4 g pro. Exchanges: 1 vegetable, 0.5 lean meat, 0.5 fat. Carb choices: 0.5.

- **1 pound zucchini, shredded**
- **¼ teaspoon salt**
- **½ cup finely chopped red onion**
- **½ cup finely shredded Parmesan cheese**
- **½ cup white whole wheat flour or all-purpose flour**
- **½ cup refrigerated or frozen egg product, thawed, or 2 eggs, lightly beaten**
- **1 tablespoon extra virgin olive oil**

Zucchini Pancakes

- **¼ teaspoon garlic powder**
- **¼ teaspoon ground black pepper**

Nonstick cooking spray
- **1 teaspoon extra virgin olive oil**
- **¼ cup light dairy sour cream (optional)**

Chopped red onion (optional)
Shredded or bite-size sticks zucchini (optional)

1. In a large bowl, combine 1 pound zucchini and salt. Let stand 30 minutes. Place zucchini in a strainer and press firmly with a rubber spatula to force out water.

2. In a large bowl, combine zucchini, ½ cup red onion, the Parmesan cheese, flour, eggs, the 1 tablespoon olive oil, garlic powder, and pepper. If the batter is not thick enough to hold together, add a little more flour, 1 tablespoon at a time, until the mixture is the right consistency.

3. Lightly coat a large skillet or griddle with nonstick cooking spray. Add the 1 teaspoon olive oil to skillet and heat over medium heat. Using ¼ cup zucchini mixture per pancake, drop zucchini mixture onto hot skillet, leaving 2 to 3 inches between mounds. Flatten mounds to about ½-inch thickness. Cook pancakes about 4 minutes or until golden brown, carefully turning once halfway through cooking.

4. Keep pancakes warm in a 300°F oven while cooking the remaining pancakes. If desired, top pancakes with sour cream and sprinkle with additional chopped red onion or shredded zucchini to serve. **Makes 10 pancakes.**

Streusel-Crunch French Toast

Make a trip to your favorite bakery to purchase the bread. Ask to have it cut into thick slices.

PER SERVING: 231 cal., 6 g total fat (2 g sat. fat), 113 mg chol., 255 mg sodium, 34 g carb., 4 g fiber, 12 g pro. Exchanges: 2 starch, 1 medium-fat meat. Carb choices: 2.

Nonstick cooking spray
- **3 eggs**
- **1 cup evaporated fat-free milk**
- **1 tablespoon sugar**
- **2 teaspoons vanilla**
- **½ teaspoon ground cinnamon**
- **¼ teaspoon ground nutmeg**
- **6 1-inch-thick slices crusty whole wheat country-style bread**
- **2 tablespoons sugar**
- **½ teaspoon ground cinnamon**
- **⅔ cup crushed shredded wheat biscuits**
- **1 tablespoon butter, melted**
- **2 cups sliced fresh strawberries**

1. Lightly coat a 3-quart rectangular baking dish with nonstick cooking spray; set aside. In a medium bowl, lightly beat eggs with a rotary beater or wire whisk. Beat in evaporated milk, the 1 tablespoon sugar, vanilla, ½ teaspoon cinnamon, and nutmeg. Arrange bread slices in a single layer in prepared baking dish. Pour egg mixture evenly over bread. Cover and chill for 2 to 24 hours, turning bread slices once with a wide spatula.

2. Preheat oven to 375°F. In a small bowl, combine the 2 tablespoons sugar and ½ teaspoon cinnamon; set aside. In another small bowl, combine crushed biscuits, butter, and 2 teaspoons of the cinnamon-sugar mixture. Sprinkle evenly over bread slices in dish. Bake, uncovered, about 30 minutes or until light brown.

3. Combine the strawberries and remaining cinnamon-sugar mixture. Serve with toast. **Makes 6 servings.**

Streusel-Crunch French Toast

Citrus Rosemary Scones

Citrus peel and fresh rosemary team up to give these tender scones a lively flavor.

PER SCONE: 173 cal., 5 g total fat (3 g sat. fat), 28 mg chol., 153 mg sodium, 28 g carb., 1 g fiber, 4 g pro. Exchanges: 2 starch, 1 fat. Carb choices: 2.

Nonstick cooking spray
2¾ cups all-purpose flour
⅓ cup sugar
1 tablespoon baking powder
1 tablespoon finely shredded orange peel or lemon peel
2 teaspoons snipped fresh rosemary or ½ teaspoon dried rosemary, crushed
¼ teaspoon salt
¼ cup butter
⅔ cup fat-free milk
1 egg, beaten
1 egg white, beaten
2 teaspoons fat-free milk
Reduced-sugar orange marmalade (optional)

1. Preheat oven to 425°F. Lightly coat a baking sheet with nonstick cooking spray; set aside. In a large bowl, stir together flour, sugar, baking powder, orange or lemon peel, rosemary, and salt. Using a pastry blender, cut in butter until mixture resembles coarse crumbs. Make a well in the center of flour mixture. In a small bowl, stir together the ⅔ cup milk, the egg, and egg white. Add milk mixture all at once to flour mixture. Using a fork, stir just until moistened.

2. Turn out dough onto a lightly floured surface. Quickly knead dough by folding and pressing gently 10 to 12 times or just until dough is smooth. Pat gently into a 9-inch circle, about ½ inch thick. Cut the dough with a 2½-inch round cutter, rerolling scraps. (Or cut into 12 wedges.) Transfer scones to prepared baking sheet. Brush tops with the 2 teaspoons milk. Bake for 12 to 15 minutes or until golden brown. Serve warm. If desired, serve with orange marmalade. **Makes 12 scones.**

Herb-Bran Muffins

Store these savory muffins in the refrigerator; reheat in the microwave on 100% power (high) for 15 seconds or until warm.

PER MUFFIN: 129 cal., 5 g total fat (1 g sat. fat), 2 mg chol., 93 mg sodium, 18 g carb., 2 g fiber, 4 g pro. Exchanges: 1 starch, 1 fat. Carb choices: 1.

Nonstick cooking spray
1½ cups all-purpose flour
1 cup whole bran cereal
2 tablespoons grated Parmesan cheese
1 tablespoon sugar
1 tablespoon snipped fresh basil, dill, rosemary, thyme, sage, or chives
½ teaspoon baking powder
¼ teaspoon baking soda
1 cup buttermilk or sour fat-free milk*
¼ cup refrigerated or frozen egg product, thawed, or 1 egg, lightly beaten
¼ cup canola oil

1. Preheat oven to 400°F. Coat twelve 2½-inch muffin cups with nonstick cooking spray; set aside. In a large bowl, stir together flour, bran cereal, Parmesan cheese, sugar, basil, baking powder, and baking soda. Make a well in the center of flour mixture; set aside.

2. In a medium bowl, whisk together buttermilk, egg, and oil. Add egg mixture all at once to flour mixture; stir just until moistened (batter should be lumpy).

3. Spoon batter into prepared muffin cups, filling each two-thirds full. Bake for 18 to 20 minutes or until golden brown. Cool in muffin cups on a wire rack for 5 minutes. Remove muffins from muffin cups. Serve warm. **Makes 12 muffins.**

***Test Kitchen Tip:** To make 1 cup sour fat-free milk, place 1 tablespoon lemon juice or vinegar in a glass measuring cup. Add enough fat-free milk to make 1 cup total liquid; stir. Let stand for 5 minutes before using.

Banana-Oat Muffins

(quick breads)

Mastering the simple art of making muffins and other quick breads is rewarding. Follow these easy steps.

1. **Preheat** the oven. Putting batter into a cold oven will increase the baking time.
2. **Measure** ingredients accurately. Use glass measuring cups for liquids and graduated or stackable measuring cups for dry ingredients.
2. **Avoid** mixing the batter too much. When you add the liquid, stir until the dry ingredients are just moistened; the batter will be lumpy. If you overmix, the bread will be tough.
3. **Spoon** the batter into prepared muffin cups or loaf pans. Pouring the batter will cause it to deflate.
4. **Position** the oven rack in the center of the oven and place the bread in the center of the rack.
5. **Check** muffins and quick-bread loaves about 10 minutes before the minimum baking time ends to see if they are browning too quickly. If they are, cover them with foil.
6. **Let** muffins cool in the pans for 5 minutes and quick breads cool in the pans for 10 minutes before removing. Leaving them in longer will cause the bottoms and sides to become soggy.

Banana-Oat Muffins

Processing the oats turns them into an oat flour.

PER MUFFIN: 152 cal., 4 g total fat (2 g sat. fat), 8 mg chol., 183 mg sodium, 25 g carb., 3 g fiber, 5 g pro. Exchanges: 1.5 starch, 1 fat. Carb choices: 1.5.

- **2 cups regular rolled oats**
- **¾ cup whole wheat flour**
- **⅓ cup sugar**
- **1 teaspoon baking powder**
- **¾ teaspoon apple pie spice or ground cinnamon**
- **½ teaspoon baking soda**
- **¼ teaspoon salt**
- **1 cup buttermilk**
- **½ cup refrigerated or frozen egg product, thawed, or 2 eggs, lightly beaten**
- **1 large ripe banana, mashed**
- **2 tablespoons butter, melted**
- **1 teaspoon vanilla**
- **¼ cup regular rolled oats**
- **½ teaspoon apple pie spice or ground cinnamon**
- **1 tablespoon butter**

1. Preheat oven to 350°F. Line twelve 2½-inch muffin cups with paper bake cups; set aside. Place the 2 cups oats in a food processor or blender; cover and process or blend until finely ground. Transfer finely ground oats to a large bowl. Stir in whole wheat flour, sugar, baking powder, the ¾ teaspoon apple pie spice, the baking soda, and salt. Make a well in the center of the flour mixture; set aside.

2. In a medium bowl, whisk together buttermilk and eggs; whisk in banana, the 2 tablespoons melted butter, and the vanilla. Add buttermilk mixture all at once to flour mixture; stir just until moistened (batter should be lumpy). Spoon batter into prepared muffin cups, filling each about two-thirds full.

3. For topping, in a small bowl, stir together the ¼ cup oats and the ½ teaspoon apple pie spice. Using a pastry blender, cut in the 1 tablespoon butter until mixture resembles coarse crumbs. Sprinkle the oat mixture on top of muffin batter.

4. Bake for 20 to 22 minutes or until a toothpick inserted in centers comes out clean. Cool in muffin cups on a wire rack for 5 minutes. Remove muffins from muffin cups. Serve warm. **Makes 12 muffins.**

Make-Ahead Directions: Place baked muffins in an airtight container. Store at room temperature for up to 3 days or freeze for up to 1 month.

Zucchini Bread with a Twist

Wrap the cooled loaf and store overnight before slicing.

PER SLICE: 159 cal., 6 g total fat (0 g sat. fat), 0 mg chol., 105 mg sodium, 25 g carb., 1 g fiber, 3 g pro. Exchanges: 1 starch, 0.5 carb., 1 fat. Carb choices: 1.5.

- **1¼ cups all-purpose flour**
- **¼ cup flaxseed meal or toasted wheat germ**
- **1½ teaspoons baking powder**
- **1 teaspoon apple pie spice**
- **2 egg whites, lightly beaten**
- **1 cup finely shredded zucchini**
- **⅔ cup sugar**
- **¼ cup canola oil**
- **1 teaspoon finely shredded orange peel**
- **⅓ cup snipped dried cranberries**

1. Preheat oven to 350°F. Grease the bottom and ½ inch up the sides of an 8×4×2-inch loaf pan; set aside. In a large bowl, stir together flour, flaxseed meal, baking powder, apple pie spice, and ¼ teaspoon *salt*. Make a well in the center of flour mixture; set aside.

2. In a bowl, combine egg whites, zucchini, sugar, oil, and orange peel. Add zucchini mixture all at once to flour mixture; stir just until moistened. Fold in cranberries. Spoon batter into prepared loaf pan.

3. Bake for 50 to 55 minutes or until a toothpick inserted near center comes out clean. Cool in pan on a wire rack for 10 minutes. Remove bread from pan. Cool on wire rack. **Makes 1 loaf (12 slices).**

Zucchini Bread with a Twist

(scoop it up)

One scoop of homemade granola equals pure breakfast bliss. Spiced and slightly sweet, this nutty cereal mix delivers multiple vitamins, nutrients, and fiber. Try some sprinkled over frozen yogurt, layered with low-fat yogurt, or mixed with fresh berries. Alone, it makes a great snack, too.

Honey-Orange Granola

Quick Tip:

If you start your morning with a deluxe coffee drink, do so with caution. Many fancy coffee drinks are loaded with calories, fat, and carbohydrates. Next time you order, request the smallest size and that it be made with sugar substitute, fat-free milk, and no whipped topping.

Honey-Orange Granola

You control the ingredients when you make your own granola. Purchased granola can be high in fat, sodium, and carbs.

PER SERVING: 136 cal., 3 g total fat (0 g sat. fat), 0 mg chol., 39 mg sodium, 23 g carb., 3 g fiber, 4 g pro. Exchanges: 1 starch, 0.5 carb., 0.5 fat. Carb choices: 1.5.

Nonstick cooking spray
2½ cups regular rolled oats
1 cup wheat flakes
⅓ cup Grape Nuts or whole bran cereal
⅓ cup sliced almonds or pecan pieces
⅓ cup orange juice
2 tablespoons honey
¼ teaspoon ground allspice
¼ teaspoon ground cinnamon
Low-fat yogurt, fat-free milk, or fresh fruit (optional)

1. Preheat oven to 325°F. Coat a 15×10×1-inch baking pan with nonstick cooking spray; set aside. In a bowl, combine oats, wheat flakes, Grape Nuts, and nuts. In a saucepan, stir together orange juice, honey, allspice, and cinnamon. Cook and stir just until boiling. Remove from heat. Pour over oat mixture, tossing just until coated.

2. Spread oat mixture evenly in prepared pan. Bake for 30 to 35 minutes or until oats are lightly browned, stirring twice. Remove from oven. Immediately turn out onto a piece of foil; cool completely. Serve with yogurt, milk, and/or fresh fruit. **Makes 12 (⅓-cup) servings.**

Make-Ahead Directions: Prepare as above. Transfer cooled mixture to an airtight container. Store in the refrigerator for up to 2 weeks or in the freezer for up to 3 months.

Fruity Oatmeal

Pour a little fat-free milk onto this fruit-studded bowl.

PER SERVING: 141 cal., 2 g total fat (0 g sat. fat), 0 mg chol., 151 mg sodium, 31 g carb., 4 g fiber, 3 g pro. Exchanges: 1 fruit, 1 starch. Carb choices: 2.

2 cups water
¼ teaspoon salt
1 cup rolled oats (quick cooking or regular)
1 cup chopped peach or apple
¼ cup snipped pitted dates or whole raisins
1 teaspoon vanilla
¼ teaspoon ground cinnamon

1. In a medium saucepan, bring the water and salt to boiling. Stir in oats, ¾ cup of the peach, the dates, vanilla, and cinnamon; reduce heat. Simmer, uncovered, for 3 minutes (for quick oats) or 5 minutes (for regular oats), stirring occasionally. Remove from heat. Cover and let stand for 2 minutes before serving. Top with the remaining ¼ cup peach. Makes 4 servings.

Fruity Oatmeal

good-for-you snacks

Summer Fresh Salsa

The little snacks between hearty meals help balance your blood glucose levels throughout the day. Finding nutritious nibbles that are quick to make and easy to take can be a challenge. Give these diabetes-friendly tasty, totable snacks a try.

Summer Fresh Salsa

With plenty of kick from a serrano chile pepper, this tomatillo-and-tomato medley is perfect for serving as a snack with baked tortilla chips or, another time, as a relish for broiled fish or chicken.

PER SERVING: 62 cal., 1 g total fat (0 g sat. fat), 0 mg chol., 127 mg sodium, 13 g carb., 1 g fiber, 2 g pro. Exchanges: 0.5 vegetable, 0.5 starch. Carb choices: 1.

¼ cup finely chopped red onion
¼ cup ice water
2 tablespoons white wine vinegar
4 fresh tomatillos
¾ cup chopped yellow cherry tomatoes
2 roma tomatoes, chopped (about ⅔ cup)
1½ teaspoons snipped fresh cilantro
1 fresh serrano chile pepper, seeded and finely chopped*
1 teaspoon lime juice
⅛ teaspoon salt
Dash ground black pepper
6 ounces baked tortilla chips

1. In a medium bowl, combine onion, the ice water, and vinegar. Let stand for 30 minutes. Meanwhile, remove and discard the thin brown papery husks from the tomatillos. Rinse tomatillos and chop (you should have about ¾ cup).

2. Drain onion; stir in tomatillos, cherry tomatoes, roma tomatoes, cilantro, chile pepper, lime juice, salt, and black pepper. Cover and chill for at least 1 hour or up to 24 hours.

3. Serve with baked tortilla chips. **Makes 12 servings (¼ cup salsa with ½ ounce chips).**

***Test Kitchen Tip:** Because chile peppers contain volatile oils that can burn your skin and eyes, avoid direct contact with them as much as possible. When working with chile peppers, wear plastic or rubber gloves. If your bare hands do touch the peppers, wash your hands and nails well with soap and warm water.

Turkey-Cheese Bites

Turkey-Cheese Bites

These little dazzlers make perfect party fare. To perk up the presentation, use a pastry bag fitted with an open star tip and pipe the cream cheese onto the crackers.

PER SERVING: 115 cal., 4 g total fat (2 g sat. fat), 14 mg chol., 278 mg sodium, 14 g carb., 2 g fiber, 5 g pro. Exchanges: 1 starch, 0.5 very lean meat. Carb choices: 1.

1 thin slice smoked turkey breast (about ½ ounce)
4 reduced-fat shredded wheat crackers
1 tablespoon tub-style light cream cheese
1 teaspoon low-sugar or sugar-free apricot preserves

1. Cut the turkey slice into quarters. Spread crackers with the cream cheese. Top with the apricot preserves. Roll up turkey portions and place on top of the crackers. **Makes 1 serving.**

Mini Nacho Cups

Baked tortilla chips and reduced-fat cheddar cheese help these Tex-Mex morsels fit into your meal plan.

PER SERVING: 132 cal., 6 g total fat (2 g sat. fat), 5 mg chol., 229 mg sodium, 15 g carb., 4 g fiber, 5 g pro. Exchanges: 1 starch, 1 fat. Carb choices: 1.

8 baked scoop-shape tortilla chips
2 tablespoons refrigerated avocado dip (guacamole)
¼ cup chopped cherry tomatoes
1 tablespoon finely shredded reduced-fat cheddar cheese
1 tablespoon thinly sliced green onion

1. Place tortilla chips on a plate. Spoon avocado dip onto chips. In a small bowl, toss together cherry tomatoes, cheddar cheese, and green onion. Sprinkle mixture over chips. **Makes 1 serving.**

Black Bean and Corn Salsa

To quickly thaw corn, place it in a small fine-mesh sieve and hold under running water. Drain well.

PER SERVING: 117 cal., 1 g total fat (0 g sat. fat), 0 mg chol., 227 mg sodium, 26 g carb., 4 g fiber, 5 g pro. Exchanges: 1.5 starch. Carb choices: 2.

2 tablespoons frozen white whole kernel corn (shoepeg), thawed
2 tablespoons canned blacked beans, rinsed and drained
2 cherry tomatoes, chopped
⅛ teaspoon finely shredded lime peel
10 baked scoop-shaped tortilla chips

1. In a small bowl, combine corn, black beans, tomatoes, and lime peel. Serve with tortilla chips. **Makes 1 serving.**

Mini Nacho Cups

(mix it up)

It's simple to pick from a list of healthful snacks, but if you are looking to vary your snack options, keep these tips in mind.

* Seek out foods that are high in fiber: vegetables and fruits (with the peel on, if edible) and whole grain crackers, cereals, and breads.
* Stick to lower-fat options when nibbling yogurt, cheese, and other dairy products.
* Pair protein-rich lean meat or lower-fat dairy products with complex-carbohydrate-containing foods such as tortillas, crackers, or cereal.

Black Bean and Corn Salsa

Tomato-Mozzarella Kabobs

Superfresh and remarkably tasty—
caprese salad is a treat on a stick.

PER SERVING: 105 cal., 7 g total fat (4 g sat. fat), 22 mg chol., 183 mg sodium, 5 g carb., 1 g fiber, 7 g pro. Exchanges: 0.5 vegetable, 1 high-fat meat. Carb choices: 0.

4 ¼-ounce balls fresh mozzarella cheese
Ground black pepper
8 fresh basil leaves
6 cherry tomatoes
2 teaspoons bottled light balsamic or Italian salad dressing (optional)

1. Cut each mozzarella cheese ball in half. Sprinkle lightly with pepper. Wrap a basil leaf around each mozzarella piece. On two 8- to 10-inch wooden skewers, alternately thread the mozzarella pieces and tomatoes. If desired, serve with salad dressing for dipping or drizzling over the kabobs. **Makes 1 serving.**

Quick Tip:

Although making a single-serving snack is the best way to control the amount you eat, you will probably have leftover ingredients. Freeze extra fruit to blend into smoothies, toss extra veggies into a lettuce salad, or stir extra poultry into a pot of vegetable soup.

Veggie in a Blanket

To cut the celery just the right length, use the tortilla as a measure.

PER SERVING: 118 cal., 7 g total fat (1 g sat. fat), 0 mg chol., 255 mg sodium, 14 g carb., 9 g fiber, 8 g pro. Exchanges: 0.5 vegetable, 0.5 starch, 0.5 high-fat meat. Carb choices: 1.

- **2 teaspoons peanut butter**
- **1 6-inch whole wheat flour tortilla**
- **1 6-inch piece celery**

1. Spread peanut butter over tortilla. Lay the celery on one edge of the tortilla. Roll up tortilla around celery. If desired, cut in half crosswise. **Makes 1 serving.**

Asian Cabbage Wraps

Fold in the sides of the cabbage before rolling it up.

PER SERVING: 172 cal., 5 g total fat (1 g sat. fat), 0 mg chol., 198 mg sodium, 26 g carb., 8 g fiber, 8 g pro. Exchanges: 1.5 vegetable, 0.5 fruit, 0.5 lean meat, 1 fat. Carb choices: 2.

- **2 leaves savoy cabbage or green leaf lettuce**
- **⅓ cup frozen shelled sweet soybeans (edamame), thawed**
- **⅓ cup frozen chopped mango, thawed**
- **¼ cup shredded carrot**
- **1 to 2 tablespoons bottled low-fat sesame ginger vinaigrette salad dressing**

1. Place cabbage or lettuce on a plate. Spoon soybeans, mango, and carrot over leaves. Roll up leaves. Dip cabbage wraps in salad dressing. **Makes 1 serving.**

Chicken and Peach Bites

Chicken and Peach Bites

A luscious ripe peach is the key to this delightful pick-me-up. When shopping for peaches, look for ones that have good color with no green tinges and that are firm to slightly soft when pressed.

PER SERVING: 61 cal., 1 g total fat (0 g sat. fat), 9 mg chol., 101 mg sodium, 9 g carb., 1 g fiber, 4 g pro. Exchanges: 0.5 fruit, 0.5 lean meat. Carb choices: 0.5.

- **1 tablespoon canned chunk chicken breast, drained**
- **½ fresh peach, halved and pitted**
- **½ teaspoon white balsamic vinegar**
- **1 teaspoon sliced almonds, toasted and chopped**

1. Spoon chicken into the center of the peach half. Drizzle with balsamic vinegar and sprinkle with almonds. **Makes 1 serving.**

Mediterranean Dip

Mediterranean Dip

Any flavor of hummus will do for this simple dip.

PER SERVING: 99 cal., 4 g total fat (0 g sat. fat), 0 mg chol., 247 mg sodium, 15 g carb., 2 g fiber, 3 g pro. Exchanges: 1 starch, 0.5 fat. Carb choices: 1.

- **2 tablespoons purchased hummus**
- **2 grape tomatoes, quartered**
- **½ teaspoon snipped fresh oregano leaves**
- **¼ of a large whole wheat pita bread, cut into wedges**

1. On a small plate, mound hummus. Sprinkle with tomatoes and oregano leaves. Serve with pita bread. **Makes 1 serving.**

Turkey-Asparagus Roll-Ups

The lively mix of smoky turkey, light cream cheese, and crisp-cooked asparagus in this easy fix-up is sensational.

PER SERVING: 59 cal., 2 g total fat (1 g sat. fat), 19 mg chol., 279 mg sodium, 4 g carb., 1 g fiber, 7 g pro. Exchanges: 0.5 vegetable, 1 very lean meat. Carb choices: 0.

- **2 teaspoons tub-style light cream cheese**
- **2 thin slices smoked turkey breast* (1 ounce total)**
- **Ground black pepper**
- **2 crisp-cooked and chilled asparagus spears****

1. Divide cream cheese between turkey breast slices, spreading evenly. Sprinkle lightly with pepper. Top each turkey slice with an asparagus spear. Roll up. **Makes 1 serving.**

***Test Kitchen Tip:** Choose a turkey product that is lower in sodium, such as Hormel or Healthy Choice brands.

****Test Kitchen Tip:** To cook the asparagus, snap off and discard the woody base of each asparagus spear. In a covered medium saucepan, cook asparagus spears in a small amount of boiling water for 3 to 5 minutes or just until crisp tender. Drain and rinse in cold water to cool quickly. Drain well.

Chicken Salad with Apple Slices

Stir this fruited chicken salad together and chill for up to 24 hours.

PER SERVING: 137 cal., 4 g total fat (1 g sat. fat), 34 mg chol., 102 mg sodium, 15 g carb., 2 g fiber, 12 g pro. Exchanges: 1 fruit, 1.5 lean meat, 0.5 fat. Carb choices: 1.

- **2 tablespoons tub-style light cream cheese spread with garden vegetables**
- **2 tablespoons light mayonnaise or salad dressing**
- **1 teaspoon apple cider vinegar**
- **1½ cups chopped cooked chicken breast**
- **½ cup chopped celery**
- **¼ cup dried cranberries**
- **¼ teaspoon ground black pepper**
- **3 medium apples, cored and sliced**

1. For chicken salad, in a medium bowl, combine cream cheese, mayonnaise, and vinegar. Stir in chicken breast, celery, and dried cranberries. Sprinkle with pepper. Serve with apple slices. **Makes 6 servings (⅓ cup chicken salad with ½ apple per serving).**

Turkey-Asparagus Roll-Ups

(fast fuel solutions)

When you need a quick boost and want to forgo fat- or salt-laden packaged snacks, try one of these healthful options.

1. **Swirl** a handful of chopped strawberries into a single-serving carton of no-fat plain or flavored yogurt.
2. **Add** a few fresh blueberries to a snack-size cup of ready-to-eat sugar-free vanilla pudding and sprinkle with a little granola.
3. **Spread** some reduced-sugar fruit jam on a rice cake.
4. **Smear** a little nut butter onto apple slices.
5. **Pair** baked tortilla chips with a black bean salsa. Add a squeeze of fresh lime for some extra zing.
6. **Pop** a mini bag of light microwave popcorn and add a sprinkle of chili powder or garlic powder for extra flavor.
7. **Fold** a few halved grape tomatoes into low-fat cottage cheese and sprinkle with snipped fresh herbs.
8. **Dunk** fresh vegetables such as baby carrots, broccoli florets, and sweet pepper strips into hummus.
9. **Sprinkle** just a few blue cheese crumbles over fresh pear slices.
10. **Grab** a handful of almonds.

Chicken Salad with Apple Slices

Quick Tip:

Snack mixes are the perfect munching food. But because they can be addictive, it's easier to eat more than you really should. To squelch the urge to munch on more than one serving, measure the mix into single-serving amounts and package them in airtight containers or resealable plastic bags.

Sweet 'n' Salty Snack Mix

Store this crunchy snack in an airtight container for up to two weeks.

PER SERVING: 129 cal., 6 g total fat (3 g sat. fat), 2 mg chol., 146 mg sodium, 20 g carb., 1 g fiber, 2 g pro. Exchanges: 1 starch, 1 fat. Carb choices: 1.

- **1 cup round toasted honey-nut oat cereal**
- **¾ cup bite-size whole grain fish-shape cheddar cheese crackers**
- **½ cup honey wheat braided pretzel twists, broken into bite-size pieces**
- **½ cup semisweet or dark chocolate pieces**

1. In a large bowl, combine cereal, crackers, pretzels, and chocolate pieces. **Makes 6 (½-cup) servings.**

Quick Peach Crisp

Just 5 minutes from hunger pang to hot snack!

PER SERVING: 105 cal., 1 g total fat (0 g sat. fat), 1 mg chol., 84 mg sodium, 20 g carb., 3 g fiber, 6 g pro. Exchanges: 0.5 fruit, 1 starch. Carb choices: 1.

- **1 pitted fresh peach half or cored fresh apple half**
- **1 tablespoon water**
- **Pumpkin pie spice**
- **¼ cup vanilla fat-free yogurt with artificial sweetener**
- **¼ cup lightly sweetened multigrain clusters cereal**

1. Place a peach or apple half in a small microwave-safe bowl with the 1 tablespoon water; sprinkle lightly with pumpkin pie spice. Microwave, covered, on 100% power (high) for 30 to 60 seconds or until fruit is just softened and heated through. Drain off liquid. Top with yogurt and cereal. **Makes 1 serving.**

Crunch-Coated Bananas

These crunchy-topped, peanutty treats beg to be served with a glass of cold milk.

PER SERVING: 55 cal., 2 g total fat (1 g sat. fat), 0 mg chol., 32 mg sodium, 8 g carb., 1 g fiber, 2 g pro. Exchanges: 0.5 fruit, 0.5 fat. Carb choices: 0.5.

- **⅓ cup cornflakes, coarsely crushed**
- **2 tablespoons flaked coconut**
- **2 tablespoons vanilla fat-free yogurt**
- **2 tablespoons peanut butter**
- **2 small bananas (each about 5 ounces or about 6 inches long)**

1. In a small skillet, combine crushed cornflakes and coconut; cook and stir over medium heat for 2 to 3 minutes or until coconut is starting to brown. Remove from heat; set aside. In a small bowl, stir together yogurt and peanut butter.

2. Slice each banana in half crosswise and then lengthwise to make eight pieces total. Place each piece, cut side up, on a small plate. Spread peanut butter mixture on the banana pieces. Sprinkle evenly with the cornflake mixture. **Makes 8 servings.**

Sweet Blueberry Crostini

Sweet Blueberry Crostini

Perfect as a snack, these fruit-topped toasts make an equally satisfying dessert.

PER SERVING: 170 cal., 5 g total fat (1 g sat. fat), 4 mg chol., 124 mg sodium, 25 g carb., 5 g fiber, 8 g pro. Exchanges: 1.5 starch, 0.5 medium-fat meat. Carb choices: 1.5.

- **¼ cup light ricotta cheese**
- **1 tablespoon honey**
- **½ teaspoon finely shredded lemon peel**
- **¾ cup fresh blueberries, coarsely chopped**
- **4 slices whole grain bread, toasted**
- **¼ cup sliced almonds, toasted**

1. In a small bowl, combine ricotta cheese, honey, and lemon peel. Stir in coarsely chopped blueberries. Cut each bread slice diagonally into four pieces.

2. Divide blueberry mixture among bread pieces. Sprinkle with toasted almonds. **Makes 4 servings.**

Strawberry Planks

Banana Pudding Snack

Banana Pudding Snack

Retreat to this comfort food when you're craving a sweet.

PER SERVING: 122 cal., 2 g total fat (1 g sat. fat), 4 mg chol., 215 mg sodium, 26 g carb., 1 g fiber, 2 g pro. Exchanges: 0.5 fruit, 1 carb. Carb choices: 2.

1 3.75-ounce cup ready-to-eat sugar-free vanilla pudding
6 thin slices banana
2 reduced-fat vanilla wafers, crushed
1 tablespoon frozen sugar-free or light whipped dessert topping, thawed (optional)

1. Spoon pudding into a small bowl. Top with banana and vanilla wafers. If desired, top with whipped dessert topping. **Makes 1 serving.**

Strawberry Planks

Substitute any in-season berry.

PER SERVING: 87 cal., 3 g total fat (1 g sat. fat), 5 mg chol., 135 mg sodium, 13 g carb., 1 g fiber, 2 g pro. Exchanges: 1 carb., 0.5 fat. Carb choices: 1.

2 graham cracker squares
2 teaspoons tub-style light cream cheese
2 medium strawberries, sliced
Powdered sugar (optional)

1. Break graham cracker squares along the perforation, making four rectangles. Spread cream cheese over rectangles. Arrange a few strawberry slices on each rectangle. If desired, sprinkle lightly with powdered sugar. **Makes 1 serving.**

Double Cherry Delight

A few juicy cherries turn ho-hum into yum-yum!

PER SERVING: 47 cal., 1 g total fat (1 g sat. fat), 0 mg chol., 45 mg sodium, 7 g carb., 1 g fiber, 1 g pro. Exchanges: 0.5 carb. Carb choices: 0.5.

1 3.25-ounce container ready-to-serve sugar-free black cherry- or cherry-flavored gelatin
4 fresh or frozen (thawed) dark sweet cherries, halved and pitted
2 tablespoons frozen sugar-free or light whipped dessert topping, thawed

1. Place gelatin in a small bowl. Use a spoon to break gelatin into about 1-inch pieces. Fold in cherry halves. Top with whipped dessert topping and, if desired, garnish with a *fresh dark sweet cherry.* **Makes 1 serving.**

Double Cherry Delight

Berries and Orange Cream

Berries and Orange Cream

To make an orange-peel curl garnish, wrap a strip of orange peel around a clean pencil or the handle of a wooden spoon.

PER SERVING: 69 cal., 3 g total fat (2 g sat. fat), 4 mg chol., 9 mg sodium, 11 g carb., 4 g fiber, 1 g pro. Exchanges: 0.5 fruit, 0.5 fat. Carb choices: 1.

2 tablespoons frozen sugar-free or light whipped dessert topping, thawed
1 tablespoon light dairy sour cream
⅛ teaspoon finely shredded orange peel
½ cup mixed fresh berries (such as raspberries, blackberries, blueberries, and/or sliced strawberries)

1. For topping, stir together whipped dessert topping, sour cream, and finely shredded orange peel. Spoon topping over berries. **Makes 1 serving.**

Pineapple Sundae

To easily drain the fruit, pull the plastic top back slightly and use it to hold the fruit in the cup as you drain.

PER SERVING: 96 cal., 1 g total fat (0 g sat. fat), 1 mg chol., 17 mg sodium, 20 g carb., 1 g fiber, 2 g pro. Exchanges: 1.5 fruit. Carb choices: 1.

1 4-ounce container pineapple tidbits (juice pack), drained
2 tablespoons vanilla fat-free yogurt with artificial sweetener
1 teaspoon dry roasted sunflower kernels

1. Top pineapple tidbits with vanilla yogurt. Sprinkle with sunflower kernels. **Makes 1 serving.**

Melon-Berry Smoothie Pops

Quickly dip the cups into warm water to help release them from the frozen pops.

PER POP: 18 cal., 0 g total fat, 0 mg chol., 5 mg sodium, 4 g carb., 0 g fiber, 0 g pro. Exchanges: Free. Carb choices: 0.

1 cup frozen unsweetened whole strawberries
1 cup cut-up cantaloupe
⅓ cup orange juice
¼ cup fat-free milk
1 tablespoon honey
1 cup calorie-free citrus-flavored sparkling water
12 3-ounce plastic cups
12 wooden craft sticks or plastic spoons (optional)

1. In a blender, combine strawberries, cantaloupe, orange juice, milk, and honey. Cover and blend until smooth. Stir in sparkling water.

2. Pour melon mixture into plastic cups. Cover cups with foil. With a sharp knife, make a slit in each of the foil tops. Insert sticks or spoons into the slits for handles. Freeze about 4 hours or until firm. **Makes 12 pops.**

Melon-Berry Smoothie Pops

delightful desserts

Berry Dessert Nachos

Everyone deserves a little something sweet, but some folks need to be a bit more selective than others. Next time you want to indulge after a meal, choose one of these decadent desserts—all lightened up and just right for you.

Berry Dessert Nachos

Crispy tortilla wedges are loaded with irresistible layers of fresh berries, a light, fluffy cinnamon-and-sour cream topper, toasted almonds, and a dusting of chocolate—all for only 1.5 carb choices.

PER SERVING: 182 cal., 7 g total fat (4 g sat. fat), 8 mg chol., 178 mg sodium, 22 g carb., 9 g fiber, 6 g pro. Exchanges: 0.5 fruit, 1 starch, 1.5 fat. Carb choices: 1.5.

¾ cup light dairy sour cream
¾ cup frozen light whipped dessert topping, thawed
1 teaspoon vanilla
⅛ teaspoon ground cinnamon
3 8-inch whole wheat and/or white flour tortillas
Butter-flavor nonstick cooking spray
2 teaspoons sugar
⅛ teaspoon ground cinnamon
3 cups fresh raspberries, blackberries, blueberries, and/or quartered strawberries
2 tablespoons sliced almonds, toasted
1 tablespoon chopped or grated semisweet chocolate

1. Preheat oven to 400°F. In a small bowl, stir together sour cream, dessert topping, vanilla, and ⅛ teaspoon cinnamon. Cover and chill while preparing tortillas.

2. Lightly coat both sides of each tortilla with nonstick spray. In a small bowl, stir together sugar and ⅛ teaspoon cinnamon; sprinkle over tortillas. Cut each tortilla into 8 wedges; arrange on two ungreased baking sheets. Bake for 8 to 10 minutes or until crisp. Cool completely.

3. To serve, divide tortilla wedges among six dessert plates. Top with berries and sour cream mixture. Sprinkle with almonds and grated chocolate. **Makes 6 servings.**

Pear-Rhubarb Crisp

Not only do whole grain cereals increase the fiber in this low-sugar fruit crisp, they make the topping easy to fix.

PER SERVING: 169 cal., 5 g total fat (2 g sat. fat), 7 mg chol., 55 mg sodium, 32 g carb., 4 g fiber, 2 g pro. Exchanges: 1 fruit, 0.5 starch, 0.5 carb, 1 fat. Carb choices: 2.

- **4 medium Bartlett pears or cooking apples, cored and thinly sliced**
- **2 cups sliced fresh rhubarb or frozen unsweetened sliced rhubarb***
- **¼ cup all-purpose flour**
- **¼ cup honey**
- **2 tablespoons apple juice or apple cider**
- **1 cup oat square cereal, crushed**
- **¼ cup whole bran cereal, crushed**
- **¼ cup sliced almonds or chopped pecans**
- **2 tablespoons butter, melted**
- **1 tablespoon honey**
- **½ of an 8-ounce container frozen light whipped dessert topping, thawed (optional)**

1. Preheat oven to 375°F. In a large bowl, combine pears or apples, rhubarb, and flour. Add the ¼ cup honey and the apple juice; toss gently to coat. Transfer fruit mixture to a 2-quart square baking dish. Cover dish with foil. Bake for 30 to 40 minutes or just until pears or apples are tender.

2. Meanwhile, for topping, in a medium bowl, combine crushed cereals and nuts. Add butter and the 1 tablespoon honey; toss to coat. Sprinkle over partially baked fruit mixture. Bake, uncovered, about 10 minutes more or until fruit is very tender and topping is light brown.

3. Cool on a wire rack for 30 minutes. Serve warm. If desired, top with whipped dessert topping. **Makes 9 servings.**

***Test Kitchen Tip:** If using frozen rhubarb, measure while still frozen. Allow rhubarb to thaw in a large bowl about 1 hour or until the fruit is partially thawed but still icy; do not drain rhubarb. Continue as directed.

Pear-Rhubarb Crisp

Raspberry-Oatmeal Wedges

Whether you season it with cinnamon, nutmeg, or allspice, the nutty flavor of the whole wheat-and-oat crust makes the perfect counterpoint to the luscious raspberry filling.

PER SERVING: 153 cal., 4 g total fat (1 g sat. fat), 0 mg chol., 64 mg sodium, 26 g carb., 2 g fiber, 3 g pro. Exchanges: 1. 5 carb., 1 fat. Carb choices: 2.

- **2 tablespoons granulated sugar**
- **1 teaspoon cornstarch**
- **2 cups frozen red raspberries, thawed and drained, or fresh red raspberries**
- **½ cup packed brown sugar**
- **⅓ cup tub-style 60 to 70% vegetable oil spread**
- **¼ teaspoon baking soda**
- **¼ teaspoon ground cinnamon, nutmeg, or allspice**
- **1 egg white**
- **½ cup all-purpose flour**
- **½ cup white whole wheat flour or whole wheat flour**
- **1 cup quick-cooking rolled oats**
- **¾ cup frozen light whipped dessert topping, thawed (optional)**
- **Fresh raspberries (optional)**

1. In a medium bowl, combine granulated sugar and cornstarch. Add the 2 cups raspberries; toss to coat. Using a potato masher or fork, lightly mash berries; set aside for 15 minutes. Meanwhile, preheat oven to 350°F. Lightly grease a 9-inch tart pan with removable bottom or a 9-inch springform pan, or line an 8×8×2-inch baking pan with foil and lightly grease the foil.

2. In a medium bowl, combine brown sugar, vegetable oil spread, baking soda, and cinnamon; beat with an electric mixer on medium speed until well mixed, scraping side of bowl occasionally. Beat in egg white. Beat in

Raspberry-Oatmeal Wedges

all-purpose flour and white whole wheat flour until combined. Stir in oats.

3. Set aside ½ cup of the oat mixture. Press the remaining oat mixture into the bottom of the prepared pan. Bake for 10 to 12 minutes or just until crust is starting to brown on the edges. Spread raspberry mixture evenly over partially baked crust. Crumble the reserved ½ cup oat mixture over top of raspberry mixture.

4. Bake about 20 minutes or until the top is golden brown. Cool in pan on a wire rack. If using the tart pan, remove side of pan. If using the springform pan, run a thin metal spatula around the edge of the pan; remove side of pan. Cut into wedges to serve. If using 8×8×2-inch baking pan, use foil to lift uncut bars from the pan; cut into bars. If desired, top individual servings with whipped topping and garnish with additional fresh raspberries. **Makes 12 servings.**

(berries)

Your reward will be great if you give these delicate summer fruits the gentle treatment they require.

Availability: Fresh berries really are best when the weather is warm. Blackberries are available June through August; blueberries are available late May through October; raspberries are available year-round, with a peak season from May through September; and strawberries are available year-round, with a peak season from June through September.

Storing: Refrigerate berries, loosely covered, in a single layer. Store blackberries and raspberries for up to 3 days; store strawberries and blueberries for up to 5 days. Berries can be frozen by arranging washed berries on a baking sheet. Freeze until solid, then transfer them to freezer containers or bags and freeze for up to 1 year.

Washing: Wait to wash berries until right before you plan to eat them. Blackberries, raspberries, and blueberries require special care. To rinse them, put them in a colander and dip them into a bowl of cold water (rinsing them under running water can crush these fragile berries). Allow the berries to drain. Spread out the washed berries in a single layer on a paper towel; pat dry with another paper towel.

Custard Towers

Custard Towers

Crushed graham crackers, sliced almonds, and ground cinnamon combine to resemble crunchy granola in these triple delights.

PER SERVING: 157 cal., 6 g total fat (1 g sat. fat), 137 mg chol., 62 mg sodium, 19 g carb., 5 g fiber, 5 g pro. Exchanges: 0.5 fruit, 1 carb., 0.5 medium-fat meat, 0.5 fat. Carb choices: 1.

4 egg yolks, lightly beaten
1 cup fat-free milk
2 tablespoons sugar
1 teaspoon vanilla
½ cup finely crushed graham crackers
¼ cup chopped toasted sliced almonds
⅛ teaspoon ground cinnamon
1½ cups fresh raspberries and/or sliced strawberries
1½ cups fresh blueberries
Toasted sliced almonds (optional)

1. For custard, in a heavy small saucepan, stir together egg yolks, milk, and sugar. Cook and stir over medium heat until mixture is thickened and coats the back of a metal spoon (do not boil).

2. Remove saucepan from heat. Quickly cool milk mixture by placing saucepan in a large bowl of ice water for 1 to 2 minutes, stirring constantly. Stir in vanilla. Pour mixture into a small bowl. Cover surface with plastic wrap to prevent a skin from forming. Chill for 2 to 24 hours before serving. Do not stir. (Custard will be thickened but will not be set.)

3. In a small bowl, combine finely crushed graham crackers, the ¼ cup almonds, and the cinnamon.

4. Divide one-third of the graham cracker mixture among six tall 8-ounce glasses, small parfait glasses, or small dessert dishes. Divide half of the raspberries and one-third of the chilled custard among the glasses. Layer another one-third of the graham cracker mixture in the glasses. Top with half of the blueberries and another one-third of the custard. Divide the remaining raspberries, graham cracker mixture, and blueberries among the glasses. Top each with some of the remaining custard. If desired, garnish with additional almonds. Serve immediately. **Makes 6 servings.**

Fresh Fruit with Citrus Mint Dressing

Make a luscious smoothie from any leftover fruit by blending it with low-fat vanilla yogurt.

PER SERVING: 58 cal., 0 g total fat, 0 mg chol., 3 mg sodium, 13 g carb., 2 g fiber, 1 g pro. Exchanges: 1 fruit. Carb choices: 1.

¼ cup orange juice
1 tablespoon snipped fresh mint
1 teaspoon honey
4 cups assorted fresh fruit (such as cut-up pineapple, halved or quartered strawberries, quartered kiwifruit slices, cut-up papaya, cut-up mango, and/or sliced star fruit)
Fresh mint leaves (optional)

1. For dressing, in a medium bowl, whisk together orange juice, the 1 tablespoon mint, and the honey. Add fruit to dressing; toss gently to coat. If desired, garnish with fresh mint leaves. **Makes 6 (⅔-cup) servings.**

Make-Ahead Directions: Prepare as above. Cover and chill for up to 4 hours, stirring occasionally.

Phyllo-Crusted Melon Cheesecake

Thin wedges of melon and fresh raspberries make the perfect topper for this creamy cheesecake.

PER SERVING: 137 cal., 6 g total fat (4 g sat. fat), 14 mg chol., 159 mg sodium, 16 g carb., 1 g fiber, 4 g pro. Exchanges: 1 carb., 1 fat. Carb choices: 1.

Butter-flavor nonstick cooking spray
8 sheets frozen phyllo dough (14×9-inch rectangles), thawed
3 tablespoons toasted wheat germ
3 tablespoons water
1½ teaspoons unflavored gelatin
1 8-ounce tub light cream cheese, softened
½ cup light dairy sour cream
2 tablespoons powdered sugar
½ of an 8-ounce container frozen light whipped dessert topping, thawed
3 cups thin wedges assorted peeled melon
¼ cup fresh raspberries
Fresh thyme and/or oregano (optional)

1. Preheat oven to 350°F. For crust, coat a 9-inch tart pan that is 1 to 2 inches deep and has a removable bottom with nonstick cooking spray. Unfold phyllo dough; remove 1 sheet of the phyllo dough. (As you work, cover the remaining phyllo dough with plastic wrap to prevent it from drying out.) Coat the phyllo sheet with nonstick cooking spray. Top with a second sheet of the phyllo dough. Coat with nonstick cooking spray. Gently press into the tart pan, allowing ends to extend over edge of pan. Sprinkle with 1 tablespoon of the wheat germ. Coat and layer another 2 sheets of the phyllo dough; place across phyllo in pan in a crisscross fashion. Sprinkle with another 1 tablespoon of the wheat germ. Repeat with another 2 sheets of the phyllo dough, nonstick cooking spray, and 1 tablespoon of the wheat germ, placing phyllo dough rectangles in pan at an angle to completely cover bottom of pan. Repeat with the remaining 2 sheets phyllo dough and cooking spray. Turn under edges of phyllo dough to form an edge.

2. Bake for 10 to 12 minutes or until crust is lightly browned. Cool in pan on a wire rack. Meanwhile, for

Phyllo-Crusted Melon Cheesecake

filling, place the water in a small saucepan; sprinkle with gelatin (do not stir). Let stand for 5 minutes to soften. Cook and stir over low heat until gelatin dissolves; set aside to cool slightly.

3. In a large bowl, combine cream cheese, sour cream, and powdered sugar; beat with an electric mixer on medium speed until smooth. Add gelatin mixture; beat until combined. Fold in whipped topping. Spread mixture evenly into cooled crust. Cover and chill for 4 to 24 hours.

4. To serve, arrange melon wedges and raspberries on top of the cheesecake. If desired, garnish with fresh thyme and/or oregano. Cut into wedges to serve. **Makes 10 servings.**

Melon Napoleons

Melon Napoleons

In this healthful take on the traditional layered dessert, high-fat, high-calorie pastry and filling are replaced with tempting Lemon Crisps, melon slices, and light dessert topping.

PER SERVING: 194 cal., 7 g total fat (5 g sat. fat), 17 mg chol., 111 mg sodium, 29 g carb., 1 g fiber, 3 g pro. Exchanges: 2 carb., 1 fat. Carb choices: 2.

18 Lemon Crisps (see recipe, below)
¾ cup thinly sliced 2- to 3-inch pieces assorted peeled melon
⅔ cup frozen light whipped dessert topping, thawed
Fresh or dried lavender buds (optional)

1. To assemble, place one of the Lemon Crisps on each of six dessert plates. Arrange half of the melon on Lemon Crisps on plates and top with one-third of the dessert topping. Top each with a second Lemon Crisp. Top with the remaining melon and half of the remaining dessert topping. Top each with a third Lemon Crisp.* Drop a spoonful of remaining dessert topping on each stack.

2. If desired, garnish with lavender buds. **Makes 6 servings.**

Lemon Crisps: Preheat oven to 375°F. In a small bowl, beat ¼ cup softened butter with an electric mixer on medium speed for 30 seconds. Add ¼ cup sugar,** 1 teaspoon finely shredded lemon peel, ½ teaspoon baking powder, ½ teaspoon vanilla, and ⅛ teaspoon salt; beat until combined. Add 2 tablespoons refrigerated or frozen egg product, thawed, or 1 egg white; beat until combined. Using 1¼ cups cake flour or all-purpose flour, beat in as much of the flour as you can with the mixer. Using a wooden spoon, stir in any remaining flour (or knead gently until combined). Shape dough into a ball. On a lightly floured surface, roll dough to 1/16- to ⅛-inch thickness. Using a 2½-inch round scalloped cutter, cut out dough. Place on ungreased cookie sheets. Bake for 6 to 8 minutes or until edges are very lightly browned. Transfer cookies to wire racks; let cool.* Makes about 22 cookies.

***Test Kitchen Tip:** Store the remaining Lemon Crisps in an airtight container at room temperature for up to 3 days or freeze for up to 6 months. For a quick, easy dessert, serve the Lemon Crisps alone or crumble them over plain low-fat yogurt and assorted fruit.

****Sugar Substitutes:** We do not recommend sugar substitutes for this recipe.

Grilled Gingered-Melon Kabobs

Grilled Gingered-Melon Kabobs

Other varieties of melon, such as Persian or crenshaw, also taste terrific in these gingered skewers.

PER SERVING: 97 cal., 0 g total fat, 0 mg chol., 30 mg sodium, 25 g carb., 2 g fiber, 1 g pro. Exchanges: 1 fruit, 0.5 carb. Carb choices: 1.5.

- **½ teaspoon finely shredded lime peel**
- **⅓ cup lime juice**
- **1½ teaspoons grated fresh ginger or ½ teaspoon ground ginger**
- **2 cups cantaloupe cut into 1½- to 2-inch cubes, balls, and/or triangles***
- **2 cups honeydew melon cut into 1½- to 2-inch cubes, balls, and/or triangles***
- **2 tablespoons honey**

1. In a large resealable plastic bag, combine lime peel, lime juice, and ginger. Add melon. Seal bag; turn to coat melon. Let stand at room temperature for 30 to 60 minutes. Drain melon, reserving any juices. On four long skewers,** alternately thread melons.

2. For a charcoal grill, place kabobs on the grill rack directly over medium coals. Grill, uncovered, for 6 to 8 minutes or until grill marks are visible, turning occasionally to brown evenly. (For a gas grill, preheat grill. Reduce heat to medium. Place kabobs on grill rack over heat. Cover and grill as above.)

3. Meanwhile, in a small bowl, whisk together reserved juices and the honey until well mixed. Drizzle over warm kabobs. **Makes 4 servings.**

Broiler Method: Preheat broiler. Place kabobs on the unheated rack of a broiler pan. Broil 5 to 6 inches from heat for 6 to 8 minutes or until heated through, turning once.

***Test Kitchen Tip:** If desired, use a crinkle cutter to make scalloped edges for the cubes or triangles.

****Test Kitchen Tip:** If using wooden skewers, soak skewers in enough water to cover for at least 30 minutes before grilling or broiling.

Berry-Cream Cheese Tart

Plump fresh berries perched on top of a light citrus-cream cheese filling make a showy finale.

PER SERVING: 156 cal., 9 g total fat (4 g sat. fat), 7 mg chol., 86 mg sodium, 15 g carb., 2 g fiber, 2 g pro. Exchanges: 1 carb., 2 fat. Carb choices: 1.

- **1 recipe Single-Crust Pastry (see recipe, opposite)**
- **½ of an 8-ounce package reduced-fat cream cheese (Neufchâtel), softened**
- **2 tablespoons reduced-sugar orange marmalade**
- **½ of an 8-ounce container frozen light whipped dessert topping, thawed**
- **3 cups assorted fresh berries (such as sliced strawberries, blueberries, raspberries, and/or blackberries)**

1. Preheat oven to 450°F. Prepare Single-Crust Pastry. On a lightly floured surface, flatten the ball of pastry dough with your hands. Roll dough from center to edge into a circle about 11 inches in diameter. To transfer pastry, wrap it around the rolling pin. Unroll pastry into a 9-inch tart pan with a removable bottom. Ease pastry into tart pan, being careful not to stretch pastry. Press pastry into fluted side of tart pan. Trim pastry to the edge of the tart pan. Prick the bottom and side of pastry generously with the tines of a fork. Line pastry with a double thickness of foil.

2. Bake for 8 minutes; remove foil. Bake for 6 to 8 minutes more or until pastry is golden brown. Cool in pan on a wire rack for 30 minutes.

3. In a medium bowl, beat cream cheese with an electric mixer on medium to high speed about 30 seconds or until fluffy. Beat in marmalade. Fold in whipped topping. Spread cream cheese mixture in bottom of cooled crust. Arrange berries on cream cheese mixture. **Makes 12 servings.**

Make-Ahead Directions: Prepare as directed through Step 3. Cover and chill for up to 4 hours. Arrange berries on cream cheese mixture.

Single-Crust Pastry: In a large bowl, stir together 1¼ cups all-purpose flour and ¼ teaspoon salt. Using a pastry blender, cut in ⅓ cup shortening until pieces are pea size. Sprinkle 1 tablespoon cold water over part of the mixture; gently toss with a fork. Push moistened dough to the side of the bowl. Repeat moistening dough, using 1 tablespoon cold water at a time, until all the dough is moistened (4 to 5 tablespoons cold water total). Form dough into a ball.

Berry-Cream Cheese Tart

(an apple a day . . .)

Can an apple a day keep the doctor away? With just 80 calories apiece, apples are packed with vitamins that offer antioxidant protection. They're also high in fiber (especially with the peels left on), which helps with glucose absorption. Apples are most nutritious when eaten out of hand, but they're also beneficial when baked into your favorite dessert. Choose Braeburn, Fuji, Gala, Granny Smith, Jonagold, Jonathan, Rome, or other varieties that are best for cooking and baking.

Cheddar-Walnut Apple Cobbler

Cheddar-Walnut Apple Cobbler

The whole wheat biscuitlike topper helps soak up all the spicy, sweet juices from the baked apples and cranberries so you don't miss a delicious drop.

PER SERVING: 161 cal., 6 g total fat (3 g sat. fat), 10 mg chol., 115 mg sodium, 26 g carb., 3 g fiber, 3 g pro. Exchanges: 1 fruit, 0.5 carb., 1 fat. Carb choices: 2.

- **3 tablespoons sugar***
- **2 tablespoons all-purpose flour**
- **⅛ teaspoon ground nutmeg**
- **6 cups 1-inch pieces unpeeled, cored red cooking apples (such as Jonathan or Rome)**
- **¼ cup dried cranberries or dried tart cherries (optional)**
- **⅓ cup whole wheat pastry flour or whole wheat flour**
- **⅓ cup all-purpose flour**
- **1½ teaspoons sugar***
- **¾ teaspoon baking powder**
- **⅛ teaspoon salt**
- **2 tablespoons butter**
- **¼ cup shredded reduced-fat sharp cheddar cheese (1 ounce)**
- **3 tablespoons finely chopped toasted walnuts**
- **¼ cup fat-free milk**
- **1 tablespoon fat-free milk**

1. Preheat oven to 400°F. In a large bowl, combine the 3 tablespoons sugar, the 2 tablespoons all-purpose flour, and the nutmeg. Add apple pieces and, if desired, dried cranberries. Transfer mixture to a 2-quart rectangular baking dish. Cover dish with foil. Bake for 10 minutes.

2. Meanwhile, for topping, in a medium bowl, combine whole wheat pastry flour, the ⅓ cup all-purpose flour, the 1½ teaspoons sugar, the baking powder, and salt.

Apple-Apricot Tartlets

Using a pastry blender or two knives, cut in butter until mixture resembles coarse crumbs. Stir in cheese and walnuts. Add the ¼ cup milk all at once to flour mixture. Using a fork, stir just until moistened.

3. On a lightly floured surface, quickly knead dough for four to six strokes or until nearly smooth. Divide dough into six equal portions. Using your hands, roll each portion of dough into a 12-inch-long rope. Cut two of the ropes in half to make four 6-inch-long ropes. Uncover apples in dish; stir gently. Arrange the four long dough ropes over apple mixture in straight rows about 1½ inches apart, parallel to the long sides of the dish. Place the four short dough ropes across the dough ropes on the apple mixture to form a grid. If desired, weave to form a lattice. Brush dough with the 1 tablespoon milk.

4. Bake, uncovered, for 25 to 30 minutes more or until dough ropes are browned and apples are tender. Cool for 20 minutes on a wire rack. Serve warm. **Makes 8 servings.**

***Sugar Substitutes:** We do not recommend using sugar substitute for this recipe.

Apple-Apricot Tartlets

This oatmeal cookie shell filled with colorful chunks of apple, apricots, and pineapple is a treat youngsters will find irresistible.

PER TARTLET: 138 cal., 6 g total fat (4 g sat. fat), 17 mg chol., 118 mg sodium, 18 g carb., 2 g fiber, 3 g pro. Exchanges: 1 carb., 1 fat. Carb choices: 1.

- **⅔ cup quick-cooking rolled oats**
- **½ cup whole wheat flour**
- **¼ cup all-purpose flour**
- **½ of an 8-ounce package reduced-fat cream cheese (Neufchâtel), softened**
- **¼ cup butter, softened**
- **¼ cup packed brown sugar***
- **¼ teaspoon baking soda**
- **¼ teaspoon ground cinnamon**
- **⅛ teaspoon salt**
- **1 medium Granny Smith apple, cored and thinly sliced**
- **2 tablespoons water, apple juice, or apple cider**
- **2 tablespoons low-sugar apricot preserves**
- **4 canned apricot halves, rinsed, drained, and sliced**
- **½ cup fresh or canned pineapple chunks, drained if necessary**

1. Preheat oven to 350°F. For tart shells, in a small bowl, combine oats, whole wheat flour, and all-purpose flour; set aside. In a large bowl, combine cream cheese and butter; beat with an electric mixer on medium to high speed for 30 seconds. Add brown sugar, baking soda, cinnamon, and salt; beat until well mixed. Beat in as much of the oat mixture as you can with the mixer. Using a wooden spoon, stir in remaining oat mixture.

2. Divide dough among twelve 2½-inch muffin cups. Press dough onto the bottom and about 1 inch up the side of each muffin cup. Using a fork, prick dough in several places in each muffin cup.

3. Bake for 10 to 12 minutes or until the edges of the crusts are lightly browned. Cool in muffin cups on a wire rack for 5 minutes. Remove tart shells from muffin cups; cool on a wire rack.

4. In a small saucepan, combine apple slices and the water. Bring just to boiling; reduce heat. Cover and simmer for 2 to 3 minutes or just until apple slices are softened. Gently stir in preserves. Stir in apricots and pineapple. Spoon fruit mixture into tart shells. **Makes 12 tartlets.**

***Sugar Substitutes:** We do not recommend using brown sugar substitute for this recipe.

Blueberry-Mango Upside-Down Cake

Mangoes and blueberries join forces with an extra-light ginger-and-orange cake in this modern adaptation of old-fashioned upside-down cake.

PER SERVING: 155 cal., 6 g total fat (4 g sat. fat), 16 mg chol., 97 mg sodium, 24 g carb., 2 g fiber, 3 g pro. Exchanges: 1.5 carb., 1 fat. Carb choices: 1.5.

- **2 egg whites**
- **1⅓ cups whole wheat pastry flour**
- **2 teaspoons baking powder**
- **½ teaspoon ground ginger**
- **3 tablespoons packed brown sugar or brown sugar substitute* equivalent to 3 tablespoons brown sugar**
- **2 tablespoons butter, melted**
- **1½ cups peeled, pitted, and sliced fresh mangoes and/or unpeeled peach slices**
- **½ cup fresh blueberries**
- **½ cup granulated sugar or sugar substitute blend* equivalent to ½ cup sugar**
- **¼ cup butter, softened**
- **1 teaspoon vanilla**
- **⅔ cup fat-free milk**
- **½ cup fresh blueberries and fresh peach and/or mango slices (optional)**
- **3 cups vanilla frozen yogurt (optional)**

1. Place egg whites in a medium bowl. Let stand at room temperature for 30 minutes. In a small bowl, stir together flour, baking powder, and ginger; set aside.

Blueberry-Mango Upside-Down Cake

2. Preheat oven to 350°F. Grease a 9×1½-inch round baking pan. In a small bowl, stir together brown sugar and the 2 tablespoons melted butter. Spread in prepared pan. Arrange 1½ cups mango and/or peach slices over brown sugar mixture. Sprinkle with ½ cup blueberries.

3. Beat egg whites with an electric mixer on high speed until soft peaks form (tips curl). Gradually add half of the granulated sugar, beating until stiff peaks form (tips stand straight). Set aside.

4. In a large bowl, beat the ¼ cup butter with an electric mixer on medium speed for 30 seconds. Beat in the remaining half of the granulated sugar and the vanilla. Alternately add the flour mixture and milk, beating on low speed just until combined. Fold egg white mixture into batter; spoon over fruit in baking pan, spreading evenly.

5. Bake for 35 to 40 minutes or until a toothpick inserted near the center comes out clean. Cool cake in pan on a wire rack for 5 minutes.

6. Loosen side by running a knife around cake; invert onto serving plate. Cut into wedges. Serve warm. If desired, top with additional fruit and serve with frozen yogurt. **Makes 12 servings.**

***Sugar Substitutes:** Choose from Sweet'N Low Brown or Sugar Twin Granulated Brown to substitute for the brown sugar. Choose Splenda Sugar Blend for Baking to substitute for the granulated sugar. Follow package directions to use product amount equivalent to 3 tablespoons brown sugar or ½ cup granulated sugar.

PER SERVING WITH SUBSTITUTE: same as above, except 130 cal., 17 g carb. Exchanges: 1 carb. Carb choices: 1.

Mocha Soufflés

The classic combo of chocolate and coffee flavors this light-as-air soufflé, which is even better served with fresh strawberries on the side.

PER SERVING: 114 cal., 1 g total fat (0 g sat. fat), 2 mg chol., 105 mg sodium, 18 g carb., 0 g fiber, 7 g pro. Exchanges: 1 carb., 0.5 very lean meat. Carb choices: 1.

- **2 egg whites**
- **4½ teaspoons sugar**
- **1 tablespoon unsweetened cocoa powder**
- **2 teaspoons cornstarch**
- **½ teaspoon instant coffee crystals**

Mocha Soufflés

⅓ cup evaporated fat-free milk
1 teaspoon vanilla
⅛ teaspoon cream of tartar
Powdered sugar (optional)

1. Place egg whites in a medium bowl. Let stand at room temperature for 30 minutes.

2. Meanwhile, in a small saucepan, combine sugar, cocoa powder, cornstarch, and coffee crystals. Stir in evaporated milk all at once. Cook and stir over medium heat until bubbly. Remove from heat. Stir in vanilla. Pour into a small bowl. Cover surface of mixture with plastic wrap. Set aside.

3. Preheat oven to 375°F. Add cream of tartar to egg whites; beat with an electric mixer on medium speed until stiff peaks form (tips stand straight).

4. Fold about one-fourth of the beaten egg white mixture into the chocolate mixture to lighten. Fold in remaining beaten egg whites. Gently pour into two ungreased 1-cup soufflé dishes. Place the soufflé dishes in a shallow baking pan.

5. Bake for 15 to 20 minutes or until a knife inserted near the centers comes out clean. If desired, sprinkle with powdered sugar. Serve immediately. **Makes 2 servings.**

Ginger-Spiced Chocolate Cake

Make one traditional-size cake or eight miniatures.

PER SERVING: 211 cal., 8 g total fat (1 g sat. fat), 1 mg chol., 133 mg sodium, 32 g carb., 0 g fiber, 4 g pro. Exchanges: 2 carb., 1.5 fat. Carb choices: 2.

- **2⅓ cups cake flour or 2 cups all-purpose flour**
- **⅔ cup unsweetened cocoa powder**
- **1½ teaspoons baking powder**
- **½ teaspoon baking soda**
- **½ teaspoon ground ginger**
- **¼ teaspoon salt**
- **1¼ cups buttermilk or sour fat-free milk***
- **1 cup granulated sugar or sugar substitute blend** equivalent to 1 cup sugar**
- **½ cup canola oil or cooking oil**
- **½ cup refrigerated or frozen egg product, thawed, or 2 eggs**
- **1 tablespoon finely chopped crystallized ginger**
- **1 teaspoon vanilla**
- **1 teaspoon powdered sugar**

1. Preheat oven to 350°F. Grease and lightly flour a 10-inch fluted tube pan; set aside. In a large bowl, stir together flour, cocoa powder, baking powder, baking soda, ground ginger, and salt.

Miniature Ginger-Spiced Chocolate Cakes

2. In a medium bowl, whisk together buttermilk, granulated sugar, oil, eggs, crystallized ginger, and vanilla. Add buttermilk mixture to flour mixture. Beat mixture with a wire whisk just until combined.

3. Spoon batter into the prepared pan, spreading evenly. Bake for 30 to 35 minutes or until a toothpick inserted near center comes out clean. Cool in pan on a wire rack for 15 minutes. Remove cake from pan. Cool completely. Sprinkle with powdered sugar before serving. **Makes 16 servings.**

Miniature Ginger-Spiced Chocolate Cakes: Grease and lightly flour eight 3¾-inch-diameter miniature fluted tube pans. Prepare batter as directed through Step 2. Spoon evenly into prepared pans, using about ½ cup batter per cake. Bake in a 350°F oven for 16 to 20 minutes or until a toothpick inserted in cakes comes out clean. Cool in pans on wire racks for 10 minutes. Invert onto wire racks and cool completely. Sprinkle with powdered sugar before serving. If you only have six miniature tube pans, cover and chill 1 cup of the batter while baking first 6 cakes. **Makes 8 cakes (2 servings per cake).**

***Test Kitchen Tip:** To make 1¼ cups sour fat-free milk, place 4 teaspoons lemon juice or vinegar in a glass measuring cup. Add enough fat-free milk to make 1¼ cups total liquid; stir. Let stand for 5 minutes before using.

****Sugar Substitute:** Use Splenda Sugar Blend for Baking. Follow package directions to use product amount equivalent to 1 cup sugar.

PER SERVING WITH SUBSTITUTE: Same as above, except 192 cal., 25 g carb. Exchanges: 1. 5 carb. Carb choices: 1.5.

Chocolate-Drizzled Graham Cookies

For triple-chocolate cookies, stir ¼ cup unsweetened cocoa powder in with the all-purpose flour.

PER COOKIE: 68 cal., 3 g total fat (2 g sat. fat), 14 mg chol., 41 mg sodium, 9 g carb., 1 g fiber, 1 g pro. Exchanges: 0.5 carb., 0.5 fat. Carb choices: 0.5.

- ½ cup butter, softened
- ¼ cup packed brown sugar
- 1 teaspoon baking powder
- ¼ teaspoon baking soda
- ¼ teaspoon salt
- ¼ teaspoon ground cinnamon
- 2 eggs, lightly beaten

Chocolate-Drizzled Graham Cookies

- ¼ cup honey
- ½ teaspoon vanilla
- 1¼ cups all-purpose flour
- 1 cup white whole wheat flour or whole wheat flour
- ½ cup miniature semisweet chocolate pieces
- 3 ounces bittersweet chocolate or ½ cup miniature semisweet chocolate pieces
- ½ teaspoon shortening

1. Preheat oven to 375°F. In a large bowl, beat butter with an electric mixer on medium to high speed for 30 seconds. Add brown sugar, baking powder, baking soda, salt, and cinnamon. Beat until light and fluffy, scraping side of bowl occasionally.

2. Beat in eggs, honey, and vanilla until combined. Beat in as much of the all-purpose flour and the white whole wheat flour as you can with the mixer. Using a wooden spoon, stir in any remaining flour. Stir in ½ cup semisweet chocolate pieces.

3. Shape dough into 1-inch balls. Place balls 1 inch apart on an ungreased cookie sheet. Flatten slightly. Bake for 8 to 9 minutes or until bottoms are lightly browned. Transfer cookies to a wire rack; let cool.

4. In a small saucepan, combine bittersweet chocolate and shortening; heat over low heat until melted and smooth, stirring often. Cool slightly. Transfer melted chocolate mixture to a small resealable plastic bag; seal bag. Snip a small hole in one corner of the bag; pipe chocolate on tops of cookies. Let stand about 30 minutes or until set. **Makes about 48 cookies.**

Black-and-White Meringue Bites

Alternating chocolate and white layers in these crisp treats gives added eye appeal when you arrange them in a serving bowl or on a platter.

PER BITE: 4 cal., 0 g total fat, 0 mg chol., 2 mg sodium, 1 g carb., 0 g fiber, 0 g pro. Exchanges: Free. Carb choices: 0.

- **3 egg whites**
- **2 tablespoons powdered sugar**
- **1 tablespoon unsweetened cocoa powder**
- **¼ cup granulated sugar**
- **1 tablespoon cornstarch**
- **1 teaspoon vanilla**
- **¼ teaspoon cream of tartar**

1. Place egg whites in a large bowl. Let stand at room temperature for 30 minutes. Line two large cookie sheets with parchment paper or foil; set aside. In a small bowl, stir together powdered sugar and cocoa powder; set aside. In another small bowl, stir together granulated sugar and cornstarch; set aside.

2. Preheat oven to 225°F. Add vanilla and cream of tartar to egg whites; beat with an electric mixer on high speed until soft peaks form (tips curl). Gradually add the granulated sugar mixture, 1 tablespoon at a time, beating on high speed until stiff peaks form (tips stand straight). Transfer a scant 2 cups of the mixture to a medium bowl. Fold the cocoa powder mixture into egg white mixture in the medium bowl.

3. Fit a large disposable* pastry bag with a large star tip. Spoon white mixture into pastry bag, keeping the mixture to one side of the bag. Spoon chocolate mixture beside the white mixture in bag. Pipe mixture into 1-inch stars on prepared cookie sheets, leaving ½ inch between each star.

4. Bake sheets on separate racks at the same time for 60 to 70 minutes or until meringues are dry and firm, switching rack positions halfway through baking. Cool completely on cookie sheets on wire racks. Peel meringues off paper or foil. **Makes about 80 bites.**

***Test Kitchen Tip:** Do not use a pastry bag that has been used before. If bag is not large enough to hold all of the egg white mixtures at once, pipe half the egg white mixtures at a time.

Black-and-White Meringue Bites

Jasmine Tea Cookies

Jasmine tea is a type of green tea that's been scented with jasmine flowers. It lends extraordinary flavor to these tender morsels.

PER COOKIE: 59 cal., 3 g total fat (2 g sat. fat), 7 mg chol., 38 mg sodium, 8 g carb., 0 g fiber, 1 g pro. Exchanges: 0.5 carb., 0.5 fat. Carb choices: 0.5.

- **½ cup cake flour**
- **½ cup white whole wheat flour**
- **1 teaspoon loose jasmine tea, crushed**
- **¼ cup butter, softened**
- **¼ of an 8-ounce package reduced-fat cream cheese (Neufchâtel), softened**
- **½ cup granulated sugar***
- **⅛ teaspoon salt**
- **1 egg white**
- **½ teaspoon vanilla**

1. In a small bowl, stir together cake flour, white whole wheat flour, and jasmine tea; set aside.

2. In a medium bowl, combine butter and cream cheese. Beat with an electric mixer on medium to high speed for 30 seconds. Add sugar and salt. Beat until combined, scraping side of bowl occasionally. Beat in egg white and vanilla until combined. Beat in as much of the flour mixture as you can with the mixer. Using a wooden spoon, stir in any remaining flour mixture. Wrap and chill dough about 4 hours or until easy to handle.

3. Preheat oven to 375°F. Shape dough into 1-inch balls; place 1 inch apart on ungreased cookie sheets.

4. Bake for 10 to 12 minutes or just until edges and bottoms are lightly browned. Cool on cookie sheets for 1 minute. Transfer cookies to wire racks; cool. If desired, sprinkle with *powdered sugar.* **Makes about 24 cookies.**

***Sugar Substitutes:** We do not recommend using sugar substitute in this recipe.

(private stash)

Cookies are great to make and bake and then stash away for when you deserve a treat. For most cookies, layer cooled cookies between sheets of waxed paper in an airtight container. They'll stay fresh at room temperature for up to 3 days. Or freeze them for up to 3 months. Save any extra touches such as drizzling with chocolate, spreading with frosting, or sandwiching with filling until after the cookies are thawed.

Soft Chocolate Chip Cookies

When you're in the mood for something sweet, remember these chewy, satisfying chocolate chip cookies. You can have one as a treat without derailing your diabetes meal plan.

PER COOKIE: 82 cal., 4 g total fat (2 g sat. fat), 11 mg chol., 48 mg sodium, 12 g carb., 1 g fiber, 1 g pro. Exchanges: 1 carb., 0.5 fat. Carb choices: 1.

1 cup rolled oats
½ cup butter, softened
1 cup packed brown sugar
1 teaspoon baking soda
¼ teaspoon salt
1 6-ounce container plain low-fat yogurt
2 eggs
1 teaspoon vanilla
2¼ cups all-purpose flour
2 cups semisweet chocolate pieces (12 ounces)

1. Preheat oven to 375°F. Spread oats in a shallow baking pan. Bake about 10 minutes or until toasted, stirring once; set aside.

2. In a large bowl, beat butter with an electric mixer on medium to high speed for 30 seconds. Add brown sugar, baking soda, and salt; beat until combined. Beat in yogurt, eggs, and vanilla. Beat in as much of the flour as you can with the mixer. Using a wooden spoon, stir in oats and any remaining flour. Stir in the chocolate pieces.

3. Drop dough by rounded teaspoons 2 inches apart on an ungreased cookie sheet. Bake for 9 to 11 minutes or until bottoms are browned. Transfer cookies to a wire rack; let cool. **Makes about 60 cookies.**

Soft Chocolate Chip Cookies

(ripen up)

Homemade ice cream tastes better and melts more slowly if it is ripened before serving. To ripen ice cream in a traditional-style ice cream freezer, after churning, remove the lid and dasher. Cover the top of the freezer can with waxed paper or foil. Plug the hole in the lid with a small piece of cloth and replace the lid. Pack the outer freezer bucket with enough ice and rock salt to cover the top of the freezer can, using 4 cups ice to 1 cup salt. Ripen about 4 hours.

Chocolate Ice Cream

Chocolate Ice Cream

Although most diabetic recipes call for fat-free milk, this tasty pleaser is an exception. It's important to use whole milk so the ice cream will have enough fat for a smooth and creamy texture.

PER SERVING: 124 cal., 4 g total fat (2 g sat. fat), 61 mg chol., 54 mg sodium, 17 g carb., 0 g fiber, 5 g pro. Exchanges: 1 carb., 1 fat. Carb choices: 1.

- **¾ cup sugar**
- **¼ cup unsweetened cocoa powder**
- **1 envelope unflavored gelatin**
- **4 cups whole milk**
- **3 eggs, beaten**
- **1 teaspoon vanilla**
- **1 ounce semisweet or dark chocolate curls (optional)**

1. In a large saucepan, combine sugar, cocoa powder, and gelatin. Stir in milk. Cook and stir over medium heat until mixture just starts to boil. Remove from heat. Whisk about 1 cup of the hot mixture into beaten eggs; return all to saucepan. Cook and stir for 1 to 2 minutes or until an instant-read thermometer registers 175°F and mixture coats the back of a clean metal spoon. Do not boil. Stir in vanilla. Cover and chill for 4 to 24 hours. (Mixture will be thicker after chilling.)

2. Transfer the mixture to a 4- or 5-quart ice cream freezer and freeze according to the manufacturer's directions. If desired, ripen (see tip, opposite). If desired, garnish each serving with a few chocolate curls. **Makes 12 (½-cup) servings.**

Chocolate-Almond Ice Cream: Prepare as above, except stir in ¾ cup chopped slivered almonds, toasted, before ripening.

Fresh Peach Sherbet

Orchard-ripe summer peaches or apricots and nectar make this frozen delight wonderfully sweet, so it doesn't need a lot of added sugar.

PER SERVING: 104 cal., 0 g total fat, 2 mg chol., 23 mg sodium, 24 g carb., 1 g fiber, 2 g pro. Exchanges: 0.5 fruit, 1 carb. Carb choices: 1.5.

- **¼ cup sugar or sugar substitute* equivalent to ¼ cup sugar**
- **1 teaspoon unflavored gelatin**
- **½ cup peach nectar or apricot nectar**
- **3 ripe peaches or 1 pound ripe apricots, peeled, pitted, and cut into chunks (about 3 cups)**
- **1 6-ounce carton low-fat peach yogurt**
- **½ teaspoon vanilla**

1. In a small saucepan, combine sugar and gelatin. Stir in nectar. Cook and stir until gelatin dissolves. Remove from heat.

2. In a blender, combine peaches or apricots, yogurt, and vanilla. Cover and blend until smooth. Pour yogurt mixture into a small bowl. Stir in gelatin mixture. Cover; freeze for 4 to 5 hours or until almost firm. Beat with an electric mixer on medium speed about 2 minutes or until fluffy. Transfer to a plastic wrap-lined 8×4×2-inch pan. Cover; freeze about 4 hours more or until firm. (Or freeze in a 2-quart ice cream freezer according to manufacturer's directions. If desired, ripen [see tip, opposite].)

3. Let stand for 10 minutes before serving. **Makes 6 (about ½-cup) servings.**

***Test Kitchen Tip:** We recommend Splenda granular, Equal packets, Equal Spoonful, Sweet'N Low packets, or Sweet'N Low bulk. Follow package directions to use product amount equivalent to ¼ cup sugar.

PER SERVING WITH SUBSTITUTE: same as above, except 75 cal., 17 g carb. Exchanges: 0.5 carb. Carb choices: 1.

managing your diabetes

Understanding diabetes gives you a better chance of controlling it and preventing complications. It pays to learn all you can, then develop a plan that fits your lifestyle.

An estimated 21 million people in the United States, or 7 percent of the U.S. population, have diabetes, according to the Centers for Disease Control and Prevention. An additional 54 million Americans have pre-diabetes, indicating an increased risk of developing diabetes. If you're one of them, remember that you—not your doctor, dietitian, or other health professional—play the most important role in staying healthy.

Define Your Diabetes

Your health-care team will work with you to develop a personalized diabetes management plan, consisting of healthful foods, physical activity, and, if necessary, the medication that's right for you and your type of diabetes (type 1, type 2, or gestational).

Type 1 diabetes: In this type, the pancreas doesn't produce insulin, so people with type 1 diabetes must take insulin. Treatment typically begins with an individualized meal plan, guidelines for physical activity, and blood glucose testing. Insulin therapy is then planned around lifestyle and eating patterns.

Type 2 diabetes: In type 2 diabetes, either the pancreas doesn't produce enough insulin or the body doesn't properly respond to insulin, so too much glucose remains in the blood. Many people control type 2 diabetes by following a specially designed meal plan and engaging in regular physical activity. The right plan can help people reach and attain a desirable weight, plus healthy blood glucose, blood cholesterol, and blood pressure levels. As the disease progresses, treatment may expand to include oral medications, oral medications with insulin, or insulin alone.

Gestational diabetes: This type develops only during pregnancy. Women who've had gestational diabetes have a higher risk of developing type 2 diabetes.

Develop Your Meal Plan

Adhering to a healthful meal plan is one of the most important measures you can take to control your blood glucose. Work with a dietitian to design a meal plan that reflects your individual needs and preferences. Your meal plan should also:

- Include fruits, vegetables, and whole grains.
- Reduce the amount of saturated fat and cholesterol you eat.
- Minimize the amount of salt or sodium you eat.
- Incorporate a moderate amount of sugar, because some sugar can be part of a healthful diabetes meal plan.
- Help you maintain or achieve an ideal weight.

Follow Your Meal Plan

As you start following your meal plan, you'll see that it gives you some flexibility regarding what, how much, and when you eat, but you have to be comfortable with the foods it suggests. It will guide you in eating appropriate amounts of three major nutrients—carbohydrates, protein, and fat—at the right times. Your meal plan will be nutritionally balanced, allowing you to get the vitamins, minerals, and fiber your body needs. And if you need to lose weight, it will indicate how many calories you should consume every day in order to lose the extra pounds at a realistic pace.

monitor your blood glucose

Whether you have type 1 or type 2 diabetes, it's important to test your blood glucose, especially if you're taking insulin shots or oral medication. Usually you test blood glucose before each meal. Your health-care providers will teach you how to measure your blood glucose with a simple finger-prick test, as well as how to adjust your food intake, physical activity, and/or medication when your blood glucose is too high or too low. Your health-care providers will help you set blood glucose goals. For example, the American Diabetes Association suggests a target for fasting or before meals is 90 to 130 milligrams/deciliter. At two hours after the start of a meal, the goal is less than 180 milligrams/deciliter. Your A1C level (the average amount of glucose in the blood over the last few months) should be less than 7.0 percent. To keep your blood glucose at a healthy level, follow these five important guidelines:

- Eat about the same amount of food each day.
- Eat meals and snacks about the same times each day.
- Do not skip meals or snacks.
- Take medicines at the same times each day.
- Do physical activity about the same times each day.

Your meal plan can be simple, especially if you use a proven technique to keep track of what you're eating. Two well-known meal-planning systems for diabetes are diabetic exchanges and carbohydrate counting. Your dietitian may suggest one or the other. To help you follow either system, every recipe in this book provides nutrition information, including the number of exchanges and carb choices in each serving. (Turn to *page 153* to see how to use this information.)

Track the Exchanges
Exchange Lists for Meal Planning outlines a system designed by the American Diabetes Association and the American Dietetic Association. To use the exchange system, your dietitian will work with you to develop a pattern of food exchanges—or a meal plan—suited to your specific needs. You'll be able to keep track of the number of exchanges from various food groups that you eat each day. Tally those numbers and match the total to the daily allowance set in your meal plan. (For more information, see *diabetes.org*.)

Count Carbohydrates
Carbohydrate counting is the method many diabetes educators prefer for keeping tabs on what you eat. It makes sense because the carbohydrate content of foods has the greatest effect on blood glucose levels. If you focus on carbohydrates, you can eat a variety of foods and still control your blood glucose.

When counting carbohydrates, you can tally the number of grams you eat each day. Or you can count the number of carbohydrate choices, which allows you to work with smaller numbers. We offer both numbers with our recipes.

no-calorie sweeteners

There's no need to dump no-calorie sweeteners just because sugar is safer than once thought. Sweeteners are "free foods" in your meal plan—and that's a good thing! They make foods taste sweet, they have no calories, and they won't raise your blood glucose levels. The following sweeteners are accepted by the Food and Drug Administration as safe to eat: aspartame (Equal and NutraSweet), acesulfame potassium (Sweet One), saccharin (Sweet'N Low and Sugar Twin), and sucralose (Splenda).

Basic carbohydrate counting relies on eating about the same amount of carbohydrates at the same times each day to keep blood glucose levels in your target range. It's a good meal-planning method if you have type 2 diabetes and take no daily oral diabetes medications or take one to two shots of insulin per day.

Advanced carbohydrate counting is a more complex method than the basic system of carbohydrate counting. It's designed for individuals who take multiple daily insulin injections or use an insulin pump. With advanced carbohydrate counting, you have to balance the amount of carbohydrates you consume with the insulin you take. You estimate the amount of carbohydrates you'll be eating and adjust your mealtime insulin dose based on your recommended insulin-to-carbohydrate ratio. To learn how to follow advanced carbohydrate counting, seek the assistance of a registered dietitian or certified diabetes educator.

Include Carbohydrates

Although the calories from fat, protein, and carbohydrates all affect your blood glucose level, carbohydrates affect it the most. So why not just avoid carbohydrates altogether? While carbohydrates may be the main nutrient that raises blood glucose levels, you shouldn't cut them from your diet. Foods that contain carbohydrates are among the most healthful available—vegetables, fruits, whole grains, and low-fat or nonfat dairy foods. Eliminating these foods could compromise your health.

(be a sugar sleuth)

Knowing the different forms of sugar can make life sweeter when you're reading labels and recipes. Sugar content is included in the total grams we list for carbohydrates in recipes.

- Sucrose appears in table sugar, molasses, beet sugar, brown sugar, cane sugar, powdered sugar, raw sugar, turbinado, and maple syrup.
- Other "-ose" sugars include glucose (or dextrose), fructose, lactose, and maltose. Fructose and sugar alcohols affect blood glucose less than sucrose, but large amounts of fructose may increase blood fat levels.
- Sugar alcohols such as sorbitol, xylitol, maltitol, mannitol, lactitol, and erythritol should only be eaten in moderation because they can cause diarrhea, gas, and cramping.

Be Sugar Smart

For many years, people with diabetes were told to shun sugar because it was thought that sugar caused blood glucose to soar out of control. So they diligently wiped sugary foods and sugar out of their diets, hoping to stabilize their blood glucose levels. Today, more than a dozen studies have shown sugars in foods don't cause blood glucose to spike any higher or faster than starches, such as those in potatoes and bread. The American Diabetes Association's recommendations on sugar now state "scientific evidence has shown that the use of sucrose (table sugar) as part of the meal plan does not impair blood glucose control in individuals with type 1 or type 2 diabetes."

It is important to note, however, that sugar is not a "free food." It still contains calories and offers no nutritional value beyond providing energy. So when you eat foods that contain sugar, they have to replace other carbohydrate-rich foods in your meal plan. Carbohydrates can contain a healthful amount of vitamins, minerals, and fiber. So it's a good idea to focus on whole grains and vegetables for your carbohydrates rather than sugar. Talk to your dietitian to determine a healthful way to include a moderate amount of sugar in your meal plan. Or you can sweeten foods with sugar substitutes (see "No-Calorie Sweeteners," *page 151*).

Stay Involved and Informed

Eating healthfully, exercising, and monitoring blood glucose levels help keep diabetes in check—all easier to do if you follow the plans you've developed with your health-care providers. Update them on your progress and request changes if something isn't working. And stay informed about diabetes by going to *diabeticlivingonline.com* to sign up for our e-mail newsletter. You're the one who can monitor your progress day by day.

(using our nutrition information)

At the top of every one of our recipes, you'll see the nutrition information listed for each serving. You'll find the amount of calories (cal.), total fat, saturated fat (sat. fat), cholesterol (chol.), sodium, total carbohydrates (carb.), fiber, and protein (pro.). In addition, you'll find the number of diabetic exchanges for each serving and the number of carbohydrate choices, in case you prefer those methods to keep track of what you're eating.

PER SERVING: 134 cal., 9 g total fat (1 g sat. fat), 0 mg chol., 60 mg sodium, 14 g carb., 4 g fiber, 2 g pro. Exchanges: 0.5 fruit, 1 vegetable, 2 fat. Carb choices: 1.

Interpreting the Numbers
Use our nutrition analyses to keep track of the nutritional values of the foods you eat, following the meal plan you and your dietitian have decided is right for you. Refer to that plan to see how a recipe fits the number of diabetic exchanges or carbohydrate choices you're allotted for each day. When you try a recipe, jot down our nutrition numbers to keep a running tally of what you're eating, remembering your daily allowances. At the end of each day, see how your numbers compare with your plan.

Diabetic Exchanges
The exchange system allows you to choose from a variety of items within several food groupings. Those groupings include starch, fruit, fat-free milk, carbohydrates, nonstarchy vegetables, meat and meat substitutes, fat, and free foods. To use the diabetic exchange system with our recipes, follow your plan's recommendations on the number of servings you should select from each exchange group in a day.

Carbohydrate Counting
Our recipes help you keep track of carbohydrates in two ways—tallying grams of carbohydrates and the number of carbohydrate choices. For counting grams, add the amounts of total carbohydrates to your running total for the day. For carbohydrate choices, one choice equals 15 grams of carbohydrates. For example, a sandwich made with two slices of bread is 2 carbohydrate choices. The benefit of this system is that you're keeping track of small numbers.

Calculating Method
To calculate our nutrition information and offer flexibility in our recipes, we've made some decisions about what's included in our analyses and what's not. We follow these guidelines when we analyze recipes that list ingredient options or serving suggestions:

- When ingredient choices appear (such as yogurt or sour cream), we use the first one mentioned for the analysis.
- When an ingredient is listed as optional, such as a garnish or a suggested serve-along, we don't include it in our nutrition analysis.
- When we offer a range in the number of servings, we use the smaller number.
- For marinades, we assume most of it is discarded.

recipe index

D

E

F

G

H–L

M

metric information

The charts on this page provide a guide for converting measurements from the U.S. customary system, which is used throughout this book, to the metric system.

Product Differences

Most of the ingredients called for in the recipes in this book are available in most countries. However, some are known by different names. Here are some common American ingredients and their possible counterparts:

- All-purpose flour is enriched, bleached or unbleached white household flour. When self-rising flour is used in place of all-purpose flour in a recipe that calls for leavening, omit the leavening agent (baking soda or baking powder) and salt.
- Baking soda is bicarbonate of soda.
- Cornstarch is cornflour.
- Golden raisins are sultanas.
- Light-colored corn syrup is golden syrup.
- Powdered sugar is icing sugar.
- Sugar (white) is granulated, fine granulated, or castor sugar.
- Vanilla or vanilla extract is vanilla essence.

Volume and Weight

The United States traditionally uses cup measures for liquid and solid ingredients. The chart below shows the approximate imperial and metric equivalents. If you are accustomed to weighing solid ingredients, the following approximate equivalents will be helpful.

- 1 cup butter, castor sugar, or rice = 8 ounces = ½ pound = 250 grams
- 1 cup flour = 4 ounces = ¼ pound = 125 grams
- 1 cup icing sugar = 5 ounces = 150 grams

Canadian and U.S. volume for a cup measure is 8 fluid ounces (237 ml), but the standard metric equivalent is 250 ml.

1 British imperial cup is 10 fluid ounces.

In Australia, 1 tablespoon equals 20 ml, and there are 4 teaspoons in the Australian tablespoon.

Spoon measures are used for smaller amounts of ingredients. Although the size of the tablespoon varies slightly in different countries, for practical purposes and for recipes in this book, a straight substitution is all that's necessary. Measurements made using cups or spoons always should be level unless stated otherwise.

Common Weight Range Replacements

Imperial / U.S.	Metric
½ ounce	15 g
1 ounce	25 g or 30 g
4 ounces (¼ pound)	115 g or 125 g
8 ounces (½ pound)	225 g or 250 g
16 ounces (1 pound)	450 g or 500 g
1¼ pounds	625 g
1½ pounds	750 g
2 pounds or 2¼ pounds	1,000 g or 1 Kg

Oven Temperature Equivalents

Fahrenheit Setting	Celsius Setting*	Gas Setting
300°F	150°C	Gas Mark 2 (very low)
325°F	160°C	Gas Mark 3 (low)
350°F	180°C	Gas Mark 4 (moderate)
375°F	190°C	Gas Mark 5 (moderate)
400°F	200°C	Gas Mark 6 (hot)
425°F	220°C	Gas Mark 7 (hot)
450°F	230°C	Gas Mark 8 (very hot)
475°F	240°C	Gas Mark 9 (very hot)
500°F	260°C	Gas Mark 10 (extremely hot)
Broil	Broil	Grill

*Electric and gas ovens may be calibrated using celsius. However, for an electric oven, increase celsius setting 10 to 20 degrees when cooking above 160°C. For convection or forced air ovens (gas or electric), lower the temperature setting 25°F/10°C when cooking at all heat levels.

Baking Pan Sizes

Imperial / U.S.	Metric
9×1½-inch round cake pan	22- or 23×4-cm (1.5 L)
9×1½-inch pie plate	22- or 23×4-cm (1 L)
8×8×2-inch square cake pan	20×5-cm (2 L)
9×9×2-inch square cake pan	22- or 23×4.5-cm (2.5 L)
11×7×1½-inch baking pan	28×17×4-cm (2 L)
2-quart rectangular baking pan	30×19×4.5-cm (3 L)
13×9×2-inch baking pan	34×22×4.5-cm (3.5 L)
15×10×1-inch jelly roll pan	40×25×2-cm
9×5×3-inch loaf pan	23×13×8-cm (2 L)
2-quart casserole	2 L

U.S. / Standard Metric Equivalents

⅛ teaspoon = 0.5 ml
¼ teaspoon = 1 ml
½ teaspoon = 2 ml
1 teaspoon = 5 ml
1 tablespoon = 15 ml
2 tablespoons = 25 ml
¼ cup = 2 fluid ounces = 50 ml
⅓ cup = 3 fluid ounces = 75 ml
½ cup = 4 fluid ounces = 125 ml
⅔ cup = 5 fluid ounces = 150 ml
¾ cup = 6 fluid ounces = 175 ml
1 cup = 8 fluid ounces = 250 ml
2 cups = 1 pint = 500 ml
1 quart = 1 litre